SERVANTS
OF THE
- KING -

SERVANTS OF THE -KING-

KESWICK MINISTRY

Philip Hacking on Philippians
Chuck Smith on Ephesians 1 and 2
PLUS many other messages

Edited by David Porter

STL Books
PO Box 48, Bromley, Kent, England
PO Box 28, Waynesboro, Georgia, USA

Keswick Convention Council, England

Cover photos: The Rev. Canon K.W. Coates, BA
(Used by kind permission.)

British Library Cataloguing in Publication Data

Servants of the king: keswick ministry, 1989.
I.   Porter, David, *1945*- II. Keswick Convention
    Council 220.6

ISBN 1 85078 063 3

STL Books are published by Send The Light
(Operation Mobilisation), PO Box 48, Bromley, Kent,
England.
Production and printing by
Nuprint Ltd, Harpenden, Herts, AL5 4SE.

CONTENTS

INTRODUCTION

by Rev. Philip Hacking
(Chairman of the Keswick Convention Council)

Every year at Keswick is special. In 1988 we could record the great storm and liken it to the wind of the Spirit. 1989 must have been one of the warmest Conventions within living memory, enabling the thousands of Convention-goers to enjoy some holiday as well as the ministry of God's word. Perhaps therefore the 1989 theme is one of warmth, basking in the sunshine of God's love and care.

But that would be simplistic. As ever there was much challenge in the preaching from the platform, as the following pages should indicate.

The theme of servanthood came particularly from the first week's Bible Readings in Philippians, where we are all exhorted to follow in the pattern not only of Paul, the willing slave of Christ Jesus, but our Lord Himself willing to become a servant for us.

Yet the servant theme was not limited to those Bible Readings. In many ways the talks remind us of the obligation of the servant to follow in the way of the Master, demanding though that may be.

Once more this last year saw many people making commitment to the challenge of Christian service. The old

Missionary Meeting has somewhat changed its format but the essence remains the same.

There was a moving moment in 1989 when a young lady from China led us in prayer for her own country just after the grim events that had happened in Peking. Somehow that cast a beneficial shadow across the whole gathering, reminding us of the costliness of following a servant Saviour.

Regular readers of the Keswick addresses will find names of speakers well known in the following pages and some who are new. It is our constant joy at Keswick to make this blend, and equally it will be obvious to perceptive readers that though the themes of Keswick do not change, we do seek to make the message contemporary and relevant to the world of today.

God has blessed the thrust of the Keswick ministry and we are wise to keep to these old paths. But there is ever a danger that we mouth truths without really understanding their relevance. We who speak pray that somehow by the Spirit of God these ancient truths will stand out in stark reality for our challenging world. They will bring both encouragement and rebuke and will be found in abundant measure in these pages.

I believe it is one of the marks of contemporary preaching that there is a greater use of humour. It is difficult to convey in cold print the warmth of personality, and certainly from this year's platform there was much joy. Perhaps the sunshine created a very happy, congenial spirit. Humour is a great servant but a dangerous master. Woe betide the preacher who preaches to make people laugh. But humour can bring the shaft of truth home in a very telling manner and the reader will find that highlighting many passages in the Keswick sermons of 1989.

Yet it is all in the service of serious business. Serving the King is a privilege and a joy, but what a responsibility!

May these sermons encourage us to be more faithful servants of our great Servant King.

Philip Hacking

EDITOR'S INTRODUCTION

Regular readers of these volumes will be familiar with the way they are produced, but it is important that new readers know that the Keswick book is compiled from transcripts of the addresses given at the Convention. Although the speakers have this year had the opportunity to scrutinise their contributions individually (a representative of the Keswick Council also scrutinises the whole book before it is printed), what you have in your hands must be seen as the record of spoken addresses, rather than a book designed by its authors from the outset for the printed word.

So that as much teaching as possible could be included, much of the humour and illustration has had to be pruned—a good reason for investigating the excellent Keswick tape and video library (see p.255). However, the flavour of the occasion has been preserved as much as possible, and in two particular respects: this year's speakers drew on a wealth of biblical allusion, reference and paraphrase, and often their paraphrases illuminated the original texts. I have therefore not always made quotations follow the original strictly, except where a direct quotation was clearly intended. Also, I have not provided references for every one of the numerous biblical allusions, which would have made the text resemble a commentary rather than a series of teaching addresses.

As in previous years, you are recommended to have a Bible open as you read. It will be particularly helpful in view of the fact that the addresses and many biblical quotations have been abridged, but those listening to the originals in the tent or on tape have also found their enjoyment and understanding greatly increased by so doing.

I suspect that the Editor's role in the Keswick book might be seen as similar to the great hurricane of 1987: some thinning of the trees was desirable, but everybody's view of which should have been kept and which destroyed is different. I hope I have not felled too many favourite trees. As I said earlier, for those who want to roam the forest in its untouched state, the Keswick tape and video library is available. But in this volume you will find almost all the teaching, and a good deal of the atmosphere, of the addresses that have been included.

David Porter

BIBLE READINGS:
Prisoner of Hope

by Rev. Philip Hacking

1. A Servant at Prayer
(Philippians 1:1–26)

I believe there's a very real word from the Lord to us all in this lovely letter.

My title is 'Prisoner of Hope', a phrase that comes from Zechariah 9:12. Paul was a prisoner; his letter is full of hope. We speak to a world where there are not only prisoners of conscience, but prisoners of hope. We're glad to have at least one person from China here at this Convention this week, and we remember the Chinese; many of them living with hope and yet, in a sense, prisoners.

But I believe it is so with all of us. As we listen to what God would say, may it not be just an academic Bible reading concerned only with finding out exactly what Paul says (though it's my task, under God, to draw that out); may we relate it to our world and to our lives. And we can only do that for ourselves.

Background

Now, we know Paul was in prison. We don't exactly know where he was in prison because he has not bothered to tell us, and of course the commentators disagree between themselves. Tradition says he was in Rome, and I am by nature a traditionalist, but it doesn't really matter.

But if it was Rome, then we know what it was like for Paul in prison. You can read it in Acts 28: not a deep, dark dungeon, but a rented home. But he had a soldier chained to him and he hadn't got freedom. And yet people were coming, and he was using that opportunity.

No self-pity

What is lovely about Paul in prison is that he isn't full of self-pity. When you read this letter you would hardly know he was in prison. Just the occasional reference; for example, in 1:13–14 he speaks of the chains he's in for Christ. Could we start our Bible readings, some of us, by getting rid of that pity?

Here's a man in prison and you would hardly know it. Yet he starts his letter by saying that he and Timothy were slaves of Christ Jesus and in that sense we are all slaves, or should be. Elsewhere, when he is writing to the Ephesians, he calls himself an ambassador in chains (Eph 6:20).

It's a letter from prison—yet it is also a joyful letter. If you love Bible statistics, the word 'joy' is mentioned sixteen times in 104 verses. It breathes that kind of atmosphere!

A thank-you letter

It's primarily a thank-you letter. Paul is saying 'thank you', and we'll see in chapter four why he is saying 'thank you'.

Did you as a child have to learn to write thank-you letters? Christmas was lovely apart from the thank-you letters you had to write at the end! And do you remember when people would buy you 'useful presents', like a pair of socks? Weren't they awful, those useful presents!

Well, Paul is rejoicing about a very useful present that had come from his friends in Philippi, so he's writing a thank-you letter. You won't learn a lot about Paul unless you're reading very carefully, but you will learn a lot about the church in Philippi. His letter is full of pastoral concern. He bothers about their unity and their humility and because of that, we'll see in tomorrow's reading, there's a tremendous, deep passage, with which theologians have battled for years, about the person of Jesus. Yet it's in a letter saying 'thank you' that he talks, almost incidentally, about the person of Jesus.

Preachers, can I remind you? We want to expound these great truths, but we want them to be relevant to the world in which people live. Our desire is not to make great theologians of our congregation, but to make good Christians, and we need the truth in order to help us to be the kind of people the Lord means us to be.

Philippi, Europe

Philippi was a proud Roman colony. The Philippians were citizens of Rome, and that's why in 3:20 it says 'our citizenship is in heaven'. They were proud of being Roman citizens, quite rightly so, but Paul would say, 'Ah, but our citizenship's in heaven. We are citizens of a greater kingdom even than Rome.'

It was the first place in Europe where Paul preached the gospel. Please, Europeans, British people—and we're often very proud, often wrongly—do remember, the gospel came to us from outside Europe.

I was ministering a few months ago at a Keswick Convention in Korea, and I met a group of people who were praying for the forgotten continent—and I think you may know which it is: Europe! I was moved and humbled by the sight of those Korean Christians praying fervently for the spread of the gospel in Europe. So keep humble: the gospel came *to* Europe, and thank God it was sent out again *from* Europe. But we have a challenge still on our doorstep.

Three typical converts

So to Philippi came the message, as you can read in Acts 16. And there you can read of three typical converts in Philippi. If you understand them, you grasp the feel of this letter.

There was Lydia. About Lydia it says that the Lord opened her heart. She was waiting, and the Lord opened her heart. There was a girl who was demon-possessed. She needed deliverance. And there was a tough Roman jailor who needed to have the gospel punched at him, and it was, and he was converted.

Can I suggest that all our churches ought to embrace all three of these people? And may I ask you to pray that the Lord will give you sensitivity. Don't try and cast demons out of Lydia. Don't imagine the Roman jailor will just open his heart. People come in different ways with the same gospel. All need Jesus, and in Philippi there were more than these, but these three stand as typical.

A servant at prayer

There is no doubt that Paul has a special affection for that church in Europe where he first preached the gospel. It comes out in a very loving introduction that we're looking at this morning, the twenty-six verses to which I've give the title 'A Servant at Prayer'.

Of course, Paul is always looking upwards (e.g., verse 3). But I'm suggesting three aspects of that servant at prayer this morning: looking *outward*, looking *backward*, looking *forward*. Whenever I read of Paul at prayer, I am challenged to begin to pray like this man and to pray for the kind of things this man prayed for.

Firstly,

Looking outward (1: 1–11)
Notice, first of all,

The constituency (verses 1–2)

To whom was he writing? I love the way he starts: 'Paul and Timothy, servants of Christ.' Do you notice it? You see it without seeing it. There's Timothy the young man, the sort of man who had been brought to Christ through Paul's ministry; he's just a co-slave of Jesus. They work together, and they call themselves slaves, and they call the Christians saints—and both are true. It's a letter from slaves to saints. Who are the saints? All the ordinary Christians. And they're in Christ Jesus and they're in Philippi.

Can I throw that challenge back to you? Both must be true. We are meant to live for Jesus where we are—in the culture of our day and the world where we live. I have always found tremendous help from John Stott's analogy in his book on preaching—and it's true of Christian living as well as preaching—that every sermon must be earthed at two ends, like a bridge; in the word and in the world.

I've been challenged by meeting some Jewish Christians who want to tell me, quite rightly, that they're no less Jewish because they've become Christians. Thank God, they're not Judaists; they're Jews. But they remain what they are. And you, wherever you are, are meant to live it out in Christ. 'In Me you have peace,' said Jesus, 'in the world tribulation,' and it will always be like that. Have you got a tension as a Christian where you live? Thank God, because if you haven't, it suggests that somewhere, something's gone wrong.

And the message comes to 'the overseers and the deacons'. It's right to have leadership—overseers (or 'bishops', NIV margin), deacons. Now, I care not what you call yourself. I think it's worth going back to that lovely verse where Paul is talking to the Ephesian elders: 'Guard yourselves and all the flock of which the Holy

Spirit has made you overseers [margin: bishops]. Be shepherds of the church of God' (Acts 20:28). In one verse they're elders and they're bishops and they're pastors. What do titles matter?

But we need Christian leadership. Saints need their bishops and deacons and elders and pastors. It's part of God's plan, and if God's called us to that ministry, what a tremendous responsibility and privilege!

Then comes the promise, for all their ministries: 'grace and peace'. And we'll find later that he ends as he begins, with an offer of grace. Without that we're all lost.

The context (verses 3–8)

As he goes on, Paul brings out his deep personal feeling.

I think Paul has had a very bad press. I meet people who think he was remote, unfeeling, a kind of authoritarian figure. You could not be more wrong. Look at the language of verses 7 and 8. It is the language of deep, internal emotion. That's how much he loves them. He writes similarly in 2 Corinthians, 'Look, I've opened my heart to you, why don't you open yours to me?' (cf. 6:11–13).

Now, we're all different. We express our affections differently. And that's right. Please, if you're an exuberant person who shows your affection, and you've come to Keswick for the first time and you think most of us are a bit solemn and solid—it doesn't mean to say we don't love; maybe we need a bit of you to warm us up a little! And may I say to some of us who are by nature a little bit more remote in our affection—maybe we do need to open up a little.

I want to say, as one who doesn't find the exuberant show of affection easy, I believe that as Christians we're meant to learn from Paul, with all his authority, that we should express our love for one another. I don't mind how

you do it, but I hope you do do it. There are some quite
loveless orthodox Christians around the place, and there
are some quite loveless sound churches around the place.
And here I see Paul with his pastoral heart, and because
he loves them he's so sure as he prays that they will go on
with the Lord.

Now, please notice how he's sure. Verse 6: Paul had
been around when God began it. He'd seen them listen,
he'd seen them believe, he'd seen them sealed with the
Spirit, and now he says, 'I've got a confidence that God'—
and here is an interesting verb in the Greek—'will apply
the finishing touches ready for the day of Jesus.'

That great goal—'until the day of Christ Jesus'.

But it is one thing to say, 'I am sure God will do it.'
Could Paul be certain it was ongoing? And I note what
makes him sure. His basis for confidence appears in verses
5 and 7. The evidence to Paul that these Christians were
going on with the Lord was their *partnership* in the gospel
(verse 5).

That's the Greek word *koinonia*. Do you like fellowship? I hope you do. But I wonder if you know that the
word 'fellowship' more often than not in the New Testament has got some very practical implication. They were
sharing their money, they were giving their collection.

And also, in verse 7, they were sharing with him in the
gospel in a costly way. They defended and confirmed the
gospel with Paul. They believed in the gospel, they stood
firm by the gospel and they cared about the extension of
the gospel. So Paul begins to pray reminding himself that
God is well pleased with the growth in grace. He's seen
evidence!

May I ask you to examine your own soul gently? Is
there some evidence of that in your life? Well, I trust so.

Then in verse 9: 'that it may abound more and more'.
You always feel about Paul that he congratulates you with

one hand and then thumps you with the other. He says, 'You're doing very well, brother, sister, but—more and more!' And there's a message here for pastors. There is nothing better than to say to people, 'Look, yes, you're growing, yes, but—more and more!'

There's the context. Now, thirdly,

The content (verses 9–11)

What are the things for which Paul actually prays? For these Christians in Philippi, for these who come to faith and are growing, what are the things for which he longs?

In verse 9 we find one of Paul's omnibus words— 'abounding more and more'. It means 'going over the top'. In spiritual terms I do believe all of us should be going over the top; having an enthusiasm about our love. I hope you're enthusiastic about your Lord and your love.

Verse 11: 'Filled with the fruit of righteousness.' Yes, there's fruit—'filled with fruit'; yes, there's love—'more and more'. So he prays mostly for love. Without that, all else is vain.

Our risen Lord spoke to the church in Ephesus and said, 'You've got all things going for you. Just one thing missing. You've lost your first love.' If that goes, the rest is empty. There's no point in being orthodox, zealous, if the love has gone, so love is there at the beginning. Pray for more love.

But love 'in knowledge and depth of insight'. Paul prayed a great deal about knowledge. Now, knowledge is not just intellectual understanding. It is a personal relationship. The word is used of a man and his wife—'Adam knew Eve'. It has to do with close intimate relationship.

And so Paul prays that our love may lead to a greater knowledge of God. Look up Ephesians 4:13, which describes knowledge as a mark of maturity. So 'knowledge' is partly about a relationship, but that idea of 'depth of insight' means that we know how as Christians we should live.

Isn't it interesting that there are many grey areas in the Christian life? I half envy some Christians, for whom everything is black and white. They never have any problems. Everything is either right or wrong. I wrestle with lots of greys in my life and ministry. And in those greys, how do I know how I should act? Here's the prayer in verse 10. The old Authorised Version talks about 'approving the things that are excellent'. What it really means is looking at certain choices and knowing how we should live as loving Christians and do what is best.

I learned years ago that the enemy of the best is not the worst, but the good. Most of you will not be swayed from doing God's best by being tempted to doing something utterly despicable and immoral. It could happen, but not for many of us. Many of us miss out the best because we concentrate on things that are quite good.

When our Lord spoke about the day of His return and He said, 'As it was in the days of Noah', what did He pinpoint happening in the days of Noah which He condemns? Their immorality? No—though they were an immoral generation. 'As it was in the days of Noah so it would be in the days of the Son of man. They were eating, drinking, marrying, giving in marriage...'—and I challenge anybody to prove any of those things are wrong. But, you see, they were so concentrating on things that in themselves were good, they missed the best.

Is that possible in your life? You're a good father and mother, but you are not really fully dedicated to the Lord and His service? Or it may be the other way round. You're a terribly good church person and very punctilious in what you do in church, but you don't do very well at home, you don't do very well as a father, a mother, a husband, a wife.

You see, very often we excuse ourselves that we're missing out on the best by doing things that in themselves are reasonable and good. 'Now,' says Paul, 'what I pray for you'—and he's praying for us this morning, surely—'is that as we love more and more we shall know Christ more, and we shall learn to know what's best in our love.'

Empty love can be very dangerous. John talks about loving not in word and in tongue, but in deed and in truth. When that prayer is answered, then that lovely picture at the end of verse 10 and on to verse 11 will become our experience. Please note, 'pure and blameless' does not mean 'perfect'. That waits for heaven. But we are meant to be *genuine*, people who are real through and through; the word means 'tested by the sun'. All the blemishes are revealed when the sun comes out.

Real, genuine people, tested by the sun, and filled with the fruit of righteousness. That's what we should pray for ourselves, and that's what we should be praying for others.

Looking backward (1:12–18)

What I love about Paul when he's talking about himself, as he does often in this letter, is that it's all terribly down-to-earth and honest. What he seems to be saying in this paragraph is: 'Look, what's happened to me in the past has become a springboard for what's going to happen in the future.'

Perhaps you are going through terrible times of testing. Well, without being pious and slick, there will be a day when—not that you'll be delivered from it all and then forget it all, God forbid—but you will look back and see that in the strange way God works, He's been doing something for you in these days. In the first verses of 2 Corinthians 1, Paul writes that all the comfort he found through his sufferings enabled him to comfort others. And there are people here who can minister to people in need far better than I can, because you've been that way more than I have.

Paul looks back when he talks about

Purpose through suffering (verses 12–14)

I love those three words in verse twelve: 'what has happened'. If you read the Acts of the Apostles you can find out what happened. The journey to Rome should have taken weeks; it took years. He spent more time in prison than out of it. There was a shipwreck, there was torture, there was misunderstanding, there were death threats— all these things. And he just calls it 'what has happened'!

I love it! Here's a man who believed that somehow, through all those traumas, God was in control, and he doesn't spell out the traumas because, you see, they won't be our lot in one sense. He simply wants to say, 'Whatever's happened, God works all things together for good to those who love Him', and so he says, 'Look! What's happened to me has helped to advance the gospel.'

And he goes on (in verse 13) to point out that the praetorian guard, the choice people of the Roman army, now know about the gospel, which they never knew before; because now they were chained to Paul.

Don't you see it? I mean, if he'd been going to preach at, let's say, the Rome Keswick, think how many of the praetorian guard would have turned up. Not one! But, you see, they were chained to Paul. One by one they came on duty. Have you ever had a captive audience? Paul had! You can imagine the conversation: 'I've got a little tract here...There are four things I want you to know...You must get attached to a local church...' You almost say, 'Lord, help the man who's chained to the apostle Paul'!

And the Lord did, you see, help the man who was chained to the apostle Paul, and because Paul was there they became Christians, some of them, and at the end of the letter they send greetings.

Listen! When you want to complain about your lot, do you ever ask God, 'I wonder why You have allowed me to be here, or why You allowed it to happen to me'?

I was involved in the disaster in the Hillsborough football stadium. I was present at the match, and was there trying to help counsel a little. One of our girls, who's a nurse, had sat with a lad for hours who wouldn't say a word. He was waiting to see whether his friend was dead or alive. She sat with him, she gave him coffee, she wanted to speak about Jesus but it seemed impossible to say anything. Eventually the message came that they'd found his friend and he was dead. He went to examine the body, and she went with him. He'd hardly spoken a word for hours, and suddenly he thumped the wall and he shouted, 'My God! My God! Why?—if there is a God!'

My nurse friend was able to say, very sensitively, 'Yes, there is a God. I know Him. He's changed my life and one day He can change yours.' She went on to say, 'Do you realise the words you said are the words that Jesus said on the cross? "My God, my God, why?" '

Can I say, there are moments when we feel that we're in chains—and yet God is wanting us to make a witness for Christ wherever we are? There can be a purpose through suffering, and the dark threads are part of the fabric of experience. Isn't that easy for me to say here? Some of you could say it much better, because you've known it in a way I've never known it. But the apostle Paul can say it, and he witnesses through suffering and says in verse 14 that he and others can speak the word of God more courageously and fearlessly.

It's not enough just to witness by our life. Thank God for that, but let's use the opportunity to speak with courage and fearlessness. And do you realise that sometimes, when you're going through it, you've got a right to speak which you haven't when life is going easily? Sometimes it's out of your suffering that people will listen to you.

Sovereignty over division (verses 15–18)

I love the way this great apostle has learnt to do what I call good Christian positive thinking.

There was much division. Look at the words: verse 15, 'envy, rivalry'; verse 17, 'selfish ambition, partisanship'. There were those in Rome who did speak of Jesus, but with disparaging words about Paul. 'There was envy, there was rivalry.'

Now, I want you to get it straight. Paul is not suggesting in these verses 'It doesn't matter what they preach; so long as they mention the name of Jesus I am happy.' No, no! In Galatians, Paul says that if anybody preaches 'a gospel other than the one we preached to you, let him be eternally condemned' (Gal 1:8). So always compare Scripture with Scripture.

Never for a moment would Paul gloss over some of the heresies that are happening in some of our churches today. He would battle for the truth. Note what he says here: 'Yes, they're genuinely preaching Christ. I don't like *why* , I don't particularly like *how*, but I have learnt,' says the apostle Paul, 'that God can use even that to His glory.'

I think envy and strife are still terribly rife in the church of Jesus. I stand under the Keswick banner of 'All one in Christ Jesus' and I want to testify to the great family spirit we have in the houseparty at Keswick, all different denominations, different outlooks, and all sorts of things—and yet united in our love for Jesus and His word. I know that extends among so many of you. But, let's be honest, there are those who do preach Christ who are still guilty of envy, rivalry, and partisanship, and sometimes they could be sitting in this Convention. We need to repent of it.

But may we have the apostle Paul's grace to say, 'It doesn't matter about me. Whatever they say about me doesn't matter provided they preach Christ.' If you're a preacher, please don't use the pulpit for innuendo and personal ambition, for envy, rivalry and partisanship. How easy it is to destroy others, rather than to glorify Jesus!

But Paul could actually say—and I wish I had learnt his detachment—'I care not what they say about me provided they preach Jesus.' At the end of verse 18 we see that he'd learnt to get to the stage when all that mattered was what was happening to Christ.

Do you remember that incident (it comes in Acts 15) where Barnabas and Saul had what the New International Version rather gently calls 'a sharp disagreement'? It was a bit worse than that in the original. They really had a row, and Paul took Silas with him, Barnabas took Mark with him, and they went out and it was not God-glorifying. But it finished up with two missionary journeys instead of one, and God honoured that.

It doesn't excuse the row; it doesn't say it was a good thing to have a row; but it does say that God can graciously, marvellously, overrule even that.

'Please, Lord, take away envy, rivalry, partisanship, and when I think it's happened to me and I'm suffering from it, give me Paul's grace.'—Am I speaking to somebody, perhaps? Maybe people have left your church and gone off to start something new and you're feeling hurt and sore. Well, if they're preaching Christ, just learn Paul's grace, ask for it, and if you're one of those who went out, maybe a little word of apology to the person you've hurt wouldn't be out of place.

Looking forward (1:19–26)

There are three little words in the middle of verse 20: 'now as always'. Paul's great ambition, whatever happened to him, was that Christ would be glorified, magnified, exalted. Note also the great contrast between verse 19, 'I know', and verse 22, 'I do not know'.

Friends, there are many things you and I should know as Christians. May I equally tell you there are many things we're not meant to know as Christians. What bothers me is that we often get them the wrong way round. I meet some Christians who are absolutely dogmatic about grey areas, but very doubtful about the great doctrines of our faith. What you and I should rejoice in is that we do know certain things, and nothing will sway our belief in them. But there are many things we don't know.

Glorying in the certainties (verses 19–20)

What's Paul saying? Well, he's glorying in the certainties, and he's grappling with the uncertainties.

It's not a mark of immaturity to say there are lots of things I don't know, because there are always things I won't know, this side of heaven. I am glad it is so, I wouldn't wish it otherwise. But let's look at the glory and the certainties.

What Paul *does* know is that it will all turn out for his deliverance, verse 19. The word means 'salvation', but I think he's probably talking here in terms of being brought out of his prison house in Rome with service to come. But it's the omnibus word for salvation—and please note also that he talks about its coming through your prayers and the help given by the Spirit. And the two things go together.

Do you sometimes worry about how prayer works? I mean, there is God, He's omniscient and omnipotent, what point have my prayers got? But it's through my prayers and the work of the Spirit that things happen; and because we are praying here, things may be happening in parts of the world way beyond our understanding. And here's Paul in prison; you're praying; the Spirit's at work; I believe there will be deliverance.

But Paul did have a part to play and it comes out in verse 20. Paul says, 'I eagerly expect.' That's a great athletic word; it means that he's there on tiptoe, eager to get there. It comes in Romans 8:19, where the creation is seen to be on tiptoe and Paul says, 'That's where I am. I am eagerly expecting and I am not ashamed.' All that courage, even in prison! 'That now as always Christ will be exalted in my body whether by life or by death.' Can you say that?

You see, I think the apostle Paul constantly remembered that one day some years ago he'd been holding the coats while they'd hurled heavy boulders at Stephen, and he'd heard Stephen pray, 'Don't lay this sin to their charge.' He knew that the beginning of his conversion was in the death of Stephen. Because of the death of Stephen the church began to move. And if you ask the question, 'Why did God allow Stephen to die young?'—well, I think you may get some answers. Out of the death of Stephen the church began to grow. Out of the death of Stephen Saul went through torments of conscience till he became the apostle Paul. Don't you see? Christ was being magnified in Stephen's death.

Can we please get out of that awful idea that somehow when a saint dies it's a terrible thing, that prayers have not been answered? I remember so vividly the day when David Watson, a good friend of mine, died. People said, 'Philip, isn't it sad, our prayers have not been answered!'

I know what they meant, but I said, 'No, I don't agree. Yes, I'm sad, but do you believe that David's not sad? Do you believe that God is sovereign? Do you believe [as the next verse is going to say] "to live is Christ, to die is gain"?'

Do we or do we not?

The world says that death is the worst thing that can possibly happen. The Christian says 'No'—you and I can thank God that He's magnified not only by life, but by death.

Grappling with the uncertainties (verses 21–26)

Paul can say in verse 21, 'I've got two things I hold together—to live is Christ, to die is gain.'

May I suggest you can only say the second when you can say the first. You see, a lot of us are concerned about what happens beyond, because we can't honestly say 'to live is Christ'. But when you've got Paul's absolute dedication, of course death will be gain; because in this world Christ is only seen by faith, and to be with Him for eternity—well, it can only be gain, can't it!

So 'to live is Christ, to die is gain', and Paul says, 'What shall I choose? I do not know, I am torn between the two.' Thank God, Paul, you don't have to choose! He simply says, 'Look, I want to go with Christ. I'm ready! But, you see, I also want to stay with you because I've got work to do—but I don't know which I should choose.'

Note that lovely word 'depart' in verse 23. The Greek word is used of a boat just slipping out to sea, or a tent being taken up and moved on. I want to say to you that as Christians we have a witness about death to which the world has no answer. Death is the one sure fact of everybody's life, the great unmentionable of today; and you and I have got the answer to all that. For us, if we're in Christ, it's just a slipping away, to go to sleep in Him, to wake at that resurrection.

Well, these are all tremendous truths, but Paul says, 'You see, I may have a job to do.' And I want to finish on this note (verse 22): 'If I go on living it will mean fruitful labour for me.'

I meet some older Christians who are coasting home, who really don't think things are like they used to be and fear that things can only get worse. May I point out that there is a danger sometimes with older Christians (which many of us are) that we don't have a longing to see fruitful labour being done. But here's Paul saying, 'Right, Lord, I'm ready to go, but if You want me to stay it's fruitful labour.' Or there, in verses 25 and 26, 'I will stay for your progress and joy in the faith.'

'It's not what happens to me that counts, but what happens to you.' As I end, may I point out to you that that's because Paul had lived so close to his Saviour. He was a servant under the Servant. And the Servant was obedient to death; He never thought of Himself, He only pleased His Father and gave Himself to others.

When, like Paul, you've been close to Him, your only desires will be the glory of Jesus Christ magnified and the progress and joy of others. I hope Keswick is not a time when we spend a lot of time searching our hearts in the wrong sense. We do need to do that from time to time, but God doesn't just want us to come here so that we can have a kind of experience that makes us go away feeling good. He wants us to go out with a greater desire for His glory, a greater concern for the well-being of others. And we shall see in tomorrow's Reading that we go on from prayer to action; as we pray, so we are.

May God help us to be, like Paul, prisoners of hope.

2. A Servant in Action
(Philippians 1:27–2:18)

Yesterday we looked at a servant at prayer. We saw the apostle looking outward, in his prayer; looking backward, with thanksgiving, even through suffering; and looking onward, with some things he did know and some things he didn't know. And now we're going to see,

A servant in action

In the middle of a passage to do with the fact that Paul and the Philippian Christians are servants, Paul suddenly turns to the greatest Servant of all (2:5–11).

Theologians have pored over that great passage for years, they've written reams and reams and reams about it. And yet it's not a doctrinal treatise, it's Paul saying: 'I want you to be humble, united and loving.' From where do I take my example? Paul gives us this wonderful passage about our Lord.

Paul often writes in this way. In Colossians 1, Paul gets caught up in prayer and he remembers the greatness of Jesus. And you get the same kind of challenge; that great doctrinal exposition of the person of our Lord. Or in 2 Corinthians 5, when he's talking about motivation for service, he remembers that 'Jesus was made sin for us, the one who knew no sin, that in Him we might become the righteousness of God.' Powerful theology; but it's not there simply to exercise our brains but to challenge us to go out with the gospel.

So as we look at these verses, what we shall find is the great Servant. And Paul is His servant, trying to get across to these Philippian Christians what it means for them to serve. And he wants them to have the mind or the attitude of Christ (2:5).

Isn't it interesting that Paul quite often in his writings says to Christians, 'Look at me and follow me, because I'm following Christ.' It comes in 3:17; it comes in 1 Corinthians 11:1, 'Follow my example as I follow the example of Jesus.' Do you think that's arrogant? Dare you say that to anybody? Most of us want to back away and say, 'Oh, don't look at me, look away from me, look at Jesus.'

Friends, that's really the coward's way out. We ought to be able to say with all honesty, 'Well, you're going to look at me and I believe that you'll see something of Jesus through me.' Isn't that awful? And yet we ought to be able to say it. Paul doesn't hold back from saying it.

We saw yesterday that in verse 26 he's been wondering about what the future holds and he wants to know— should he pray that he might be taken to the Lord, should he pray that he might continue in service? And in a sense he's opting—if he had to make a choice—for going on in service; not for his sake—to be with Christ is far better— but he wants to go on (note verse 25) 'for your progress and joy in the faith'. And suddenly he stops thinking about himself, and starts thinking about others.

Oh, how many of us Christians are terribly self-centred still? In our prayers, in our thoughts, it's all 'me'. Paul's concerned about them. He's concerned about one thing:

'only' one, according to the little word that's there in the Greek at the beginning of verse 27: that they should conduct themselves in a manner worthy of the gospel.

He writes the same in Ephesians 4:1—'Walk worthy of your calling.' What a challenge! That we should live the kind of life that demonstrates we are citizens of heaven.

We saw yesterday that Philippians were proud to have Roman citizenship. You and I should be proud to be citizens of heaven, but always 'conduct yourselves in a manner worthy'.

If you have a sticker on the back of your car, drive worthily of it! A car cut in front of me on the motorway once, and I did think thoughts that were not altogether worthy of the gospel! And when I saw the back of the car it said, 'Come unto me all that labour and are heavy laden.' I thought, 'My dear friend, you'll be coming to Jesus quicker than you think if you drive like that much longer!'

But we should live all our lives worthy of our citizenship of heaven. Not in a pious, other-worldly way that puts people off, but in an honest, pure, joyful way that attracts people to Jesus. So let's look at three thoughts about service. First of all,

The manner of servants (1:27–2:4)
Two things follow. First of all, servants should be,

United in service (verses 27–30)
The word in verse 27 which the NIV translates 'contending' is the Greek word for being an athlete. The picture is that we should strive, contend together, in one spirit as one man, standing firm. We're not meant to do it on our own. We're meant to do it together.

Do you work well in a team? I am sometimes asked to give references, and am asked 'Can the candidate work in a team?' Some people, sadly, good Christians though they are, don't—and should. But there is one qualification which is very important in verse 27: to be contending as one man for the faith of the gospel.

Now, there is a limit to Christian unity. I have no unity with those who deny the gospel of Jesus; it is for those who are concerned about the faith of the gospel. In that we should strive together. Jesus prayed in John 17 for unity, truth, and holiness. Never take one without the other two. There can be a unity which is not pleasing to Him at all. There can be people who battle for the truth which is not pleasing to Him at all—I think you know the kind of thing I mean. But Paul wants the Philippians to be striving together for the faith of the gospel.

'It's a costly experience,' says Paul in verse 30. 'You're going through the same struggle you saw I had.' If you know your Bibles well—and Keswick people surely must!—you know what happened at Philippi. Lydia was gloriously converted, the demon-possessed girl was wonderfully delivered. And then Paul and Silas found themselves in prison because they were making things difficult in Philippi. And Christians in Philippi had learnt from the beginning of Paul's ministry that it's a costly business to follow Jesus.

I'm so glad that in Mission '89 Billy Graham never stopped short of challenging people to a *costly* service. It's important. And these young Christians had to learn that there's a struggle (verse 29); we suffer *for* Christ and we suffer *with* Christ.

But what do you make of verse 28? Paul says that you're striving for the faith of the gospel without being frightened by those who oppose you. It's a sign that they will be destroyed but that you will be saved. Can I suggest that you read also 2 Thessalonians 1:5–10, which says the same thing. I find it greatly challenging that Paul says,

'Yes, you follow Jesus—and there'll be a cost. Yes, I've spent a lot of time in prison—because I'm true to Jesus.'

Don't think that when things go wrong it's a sign that God isn't there. Some people think that. Because they've been expecting that everything will be rosy, they've got a prosperity gospel but in fact it *isn't* going to be like that— 'Well, clearly we can't be right with God. Clearly, God's left us.'

But Paul says the opposite. Our Lord said, 'You *will* suffer.' They rejoiced they were counted worthy to suffer. And he says that there's a sense in which it reminds us there's a final judgement day when the tables will be turned: 'They will be destroyed...you will be saved.'

Thessalonians talks about 'eternal destruction', and I have to say that I believe we must never lose the solemnity of hell and the awesomeness of what that means. If you make that destruction less than eternal, I think you make the salvation less than eternal. I do not believe you can have one without the other. No Christian rejoices that people are suffering in hell; of course not. But every Christian taking the word of God seriously and challenged by it must recognise there is that dual final end.

The persecution only reminds you that God is sovereignly in charge. You expect to suffer, but, thank God, one day the final judgement will be absolutely just. And if I were talking to people being persecuted today, they would know exactly what I was saying. Some of us perhaps find it easy. They understand.

Secondly,

United in spirit (2:1–4)

In verse 2 Paul says 'Make my joy complete.'

Isn't that terrific? Here he is in prison. Here he is chained to a Roman soldier and he says, 'I am really pretty happy, but I just want you to make my joy complete.'

I wonder where you are happiest? Lovely Christian fellowship...marvellous holiday...lovely family life... good wife...all these things. If you were in prison, separated from your Christian friends, would you ever be able to have joy complete? Yes, some of you can say, 'Preacher, I can testify to it, thank God.'

But what Paul is saying makes his joy complete comes out in chapter 2 verse 1: that they enjoy the unity that comes from the Trinity; encouragement from Christ, comfort from love, fellowship of the Spirit. Very much like 2 Corinthians 13, where Paul speaks of the encouragement, consolation and fellowship of being related to God, Father, Son and Spirit.

That's our unity. And you don't make unity; you maintain it. There's a great difference. 'Now,' says Paul in verse 2, 'all that is yours, so show that you're different.' That's the challenge of verse 2: we've got to show it by being like-minded.

'Like-minded' does not mean that Christians always agree about everything or that if you don't dot every 'i' of mine and cross every 't' of mine then you're not a Christian. There are some very narrow-minded Christians!

No, it doesn't mean that. But it does mean that in the essence, concern and purpose of the gospel, in the Spirit we are one: 'like-souled', matching heart with heart.

Do you sense it here at Keswick? You come from different traditions. Are your traditions so big you can't be like-souled with anybody who is not exactly going your way? God make us bigger than those things! There's that lovely picture. In unison together.

But also in harmony: 'Do nothing out of selfish ambition or vain conceit; in humility consider others better than yourselves.'

A church is not meant to be always in unison. I think the joy of Christian unity is that we don't all sing the same note, but that we blend beautifully together and our lives are harmonious. I wish the world could hear the church not just singing hymns in harmony but living lives in harmony. Wouldn't it be wonderful if we could portray to the world the reality of heaven by the fact that when they see us, they recognise something that's out of this world? We could actually demonstrate the joy of heaven by our unity together.

What kills it? Go back to verse 3: 'Do nothing out of selfish ambition or vain conceit, but in humility consider others better than yourselves.' In a minute he's going to give the supreme example.

Did you know that word 'selfish ambition' is one of the works of the flesh in Galatians 5? There are fifteen works of the flesh. Three of them have to do with sexual immorality. They head the list, and that's very important. Two of them have to do with the occult, witchcraft—the occult— and that's a real thing too. The last two are about drunkenness and orgies—I'm sure all of us would include those straight away. Eight of the fifteen (more than half) are pride, selfish ambition, envy, rivalry...

Are you as bothered about them? Do you really believe that if our nation needs a turning back to God, it may have to start not just with the people who are involved in the occult, grim though that is, nor just those who have sinned sexually, sad though that is? It may have to start with Christians who with all their piety are envious, proud and display selfish ambition.

It wasn't any different then. Paul wants to get them in harmony, so he thinks of Jesus, and in a moment we turn to that lovely passage.

Well now, we've looked at the manner of servants. I want now to talk about:

The model for servants (2: 5–11)

We've come to this terrific passage, the picture of Jesus.

I hope it's obvious that our Lord in Scripture is an *example*. In John's Gospel he says: 'I, your Lord and Teacher, have washed your feet, you should also wash one another's feet. I have set you an example that you should do as I have done for you' (Jn 13:14–15).

But never dissociate that from His saving ministry. He's not an example rather than a Saviour, He's an example because He is a Saviour. And because He's the Good Shepherd who lays His life down for the sheep, He is a pattern for all shepherds. And because all this tremendous truth is true, then He's a challenge to us.

The moment you bring Jesus down from this unique pedestal, the moment you make Him less than fully divine, you have robbed the cross of all its meaning, you have denuded Scripture of all its truth, and there is no example any more. The more you think of Him, the more wonderful is the cross.

Charles Wesley wrote those great words:

> 'Tis mystery all,
> The Immortal dies.

If you understand that, well, you're too good to be true! You don't understand it. No more than I do. But I know it to be true; and it's because it is true and these verses are true, that He becomes an example.

Let me drive the point home. If the Son of God left heaven's glory behind and went through all the agony of a cross for us—for me—what price my petty prides?

There are some of us who go around bearing grudges and grievances: 'I'm not understood in my church, I'm not appreciated, it wasn't my fault, they were the people who did it wrong, it's up to them to make the first move.' Oh yes? Will you bring it back to the foot of this Jesus and say to Him, 'All right, Jesus, you left all that for me, but—you understand—it's different for me'?

The more we thought of Jesus, the less we'd hold on to our petty prides.

Just see two things:

The way to the cross (verses 5–8)

He was in the very nature God, He was God through and through. Our Lord Himself says, 'Whoever has seen me has seen the Father' (Jn 14:9). What terrific words those were! And Colossians 1:15, 'He is the image of the invisible God.' He is God in a way that we can see and understand, and He is God through and through.

And yet 'He didn't consider equality with God a thing to be grasped.' That's a complex verse. If I were giving a lecture to theological students, I'd have to take a lot of time over it. But what I take it to mean is that He who was equal with God didn't hold it to Himself.

It's the picture of a child who won't share his toy. 'It's mine, it's mine and I'm going to hold it to myself.' Is that not true of some of us so-called mature Christians?

But Jesus, who in nature was God through and through, didn't keep it to Himself. He laid it on one side and (verse 7) He 'made himself nothing'. He emptied Himself.

What a terrific truth! It does not mean that He wasn't God any more; He was always saying that He was. He was still God, but He left behind—what? Some of the trappings of Deity? You see, He knew what it was to suffer, He knew what it was to be hungry, He knew what it was to have pain, He knew what it was to die. God cannot die. Jesus did. In that sense He laid behind something of the glory of heaven. And when He came to earth—here's a terrific truth!—He wasn't just a man. He became a baby, in a virgin's womb.

I believe in the virgin birth absolutely, but apart from that, do remember He was just an ordinary baby. He came with all the trustfulness and helplessness of a baby. I sometimes say that I find the second coming of Jesus easier to believe in than the first coming. If you asked me to write the scenario of God coming to earth, I'd write the second coming—majesty, angels, choirs, trumpets. That's what I'd expect to happen. But a baby, in a stable, in Palestine? Come off it!

Well, I believe it, of course. And here's the amazing grace and love. He chose to come that way, to become a man and then (verse 8) He went even further. He humbled Himself, and became obedient to death, even death on a cross.

Two simple things. In the Epistle to the Hebrews the writer says that Jesus learned obedience through the things that He suffered (5:7–8). He became obedient to death.

Enter into all that that means. Let your mind be blown by it. In all His real humanity, the Son of God was learning obedience. He was doing His Father's will, and when in the Garden of Gethsemane He cried out as He sweated great drops of blood, 'If it's possible take this cup from Me,' He meant it. In all His humanity He meant it, but then He also meant 'Nevertheless not My will, but Yours, be done.'

He was obedient. What price your obedience?

He was willing to be obedient to death, even death on a cross—and not only obedient to the cruelty but to the stigma. Paul had a battle with that. Anybody who died on a cross was cursed; and how could Messiah be cursed? Then the truth dawned upon Paul, it's recorded in Galatians 3:13: 'He redeemed us from the curse of the law, having become a curse for us.' Praise the Lord! It was a turning point in Saul's mental conversion. He understood. Jesus was cursed, but He was cursed so that we might never be cursed. And Jesus did this all willingly. He laid down His life for us.

You all know this. But I wonder how deep it all goes, that knowledge of it? The eternal Son of God becoming a baby, obedient to death, dying on a cross, stigmatised for us, cursed for us. Are we content to say, 'Thank You, Lord'? Or do we go a stage further and say, 'Thank You, Lord; I am not worthy but I want that to be not only my salvation, but my example; and I will no more cling to the things that are mine. I am willing to sacrifice, to give myself since You gave Yourself for me.'

That's what Paul's talking about. You could be a very orthodox theologian and a very bad Christian.

The way to the crown (verses 9–11)

There is a lovely 'therefore' in verse 9. Because Christ was obedient God is exalted.

Please get excited! The Greek word 'exalted' is the same word as the word 'lifted up'. 'I, if I be lifted up, will draw all men to myself.' He was lifted up on the cross and He was lifted up to glory—and the principle remains the same. No cross, no crown. If you don't want the fellowship of His sufferings, you cannot know the power of His resurrection. He was exalted back to heaven, given that name at which every knee will bow, the name Jesus.

Paul is not saying that everybody will get to heaven. But he is saying that Jesus will be sovereign over all.

The mission of servants (2:12–18)

God's 'therefore' in verse 9 becomes our 'therefore' in verse 12.

I love the way Paul blends deep theology with a practical challenge, so that we can go out of this tent not just

with brows furrowed saying, 'It's great theology, marvellous truth,' but with feet itching to go out and do
something about it.

Two practical challenges, then:

Work out (verses 12–15)

Note verse 12: 'Obey not just in my presence only, but
even more in my absence.'

Some of us are not bad Christians when other people
are watching. We're not quite so good when they're not
watching—and He's always watching. He doesn't just
have His video on us when we're here in Keswick or in
church, it's always there on us. So the challenge is, work it
out!

I find it very exciting. Because, you see, first of all, our
salvation is not by works but by grace through faith. But
we are still created in Christ Jesus unto good works, and
so we are told to work out our salvation (verse 13)—God
works in and we work out. Just two things about it.

Please note, it's clear in the Greek, work out your *own*
salvation. I'm a great believer in the body of Christ; none
of us live to ourselves alone. We all need others. But I fear
that the doctrine is getting lost of the great independence
of a Christian. In 1 Thessalonians, Paul says that we
should be dependent on nobody. You work out your own
salvation. Nobody else can do it for you. You'll need the
help and prayers of others, but you work it out on your
own. We're to bear each other's burdens, says Galatians
6. But each one of us must bear our own load. Work it
out, your own salvation.

The other thing to note in verse 12 is 'with fear and
trembling'. Have we lost our sense of awe?

Some people think 'awe and trembling' means for
example that we all come to church and sit there quietly
for the first half-hour before the church starts, and nobody

says a word. That's not necessarily reverence and awe. You could be fast asleep—it could have nothing to do with awe and reverence whatever. And I have to say, I'd rather my congregation was anticipating the next hour with some excitement than sitting there solemnly thinking, 'Dear me, when will all this be over?' Awe does not necessarily mean quiet and reverence.

Paul talks about the fear of Christ in 2 Corinthians 5:11 and a sense of awe before a Jesus who did all this for me. And if I really believe verses 5 to 11 of Philippians 2, there'll be a great deal of awe about how I work out my own salvation.

But look at verse 14. There is to be a quality of life as well as a quality of work: 'Do everything without complaining or arguing.' Now, there's a text for you to put on your wall for today.

Are you a grumbler? I think it's one of the patterns of this world that most people start the day with grumbling. We're never satisfied. We are grumblers, many of us, by nature.

Those of you who know me well will know I love the Greek word for grumbling: *gongusmōn*. It's a marvellous, onomatopoeic word, *gong-goos-moan*. The churches are full of *gong-goos-moaning* Christians—'It's not like it used to be, it's not like it should be.'

Now of course we've a right to speak out—of course there are many things that are wrong. This passage doesn't say we should keep our mouths shut all the time, but what it does say is that our spirit should be gratitude, not grumbling. The Bible is full of thanksgiving, not grumbling and complaining.

There's a lot in the New Testament about the dangers of grumbling causing controversies. The Jews in the wilderness were always grumbling. They forgot. Do you remember how in the wilderness they grumbled because they got fed up with the manna? 'Oh, can't you give us something better? Manna, all these years? And they forgot how gloriously they had been redeemed.

When next you grumble, stop and say 'Thank You, Lord, for all You've done.' And if you think you have a right to grumble at your minister, your friend or whatever, first of all just say 'thank you' for the things that you can say 'thank you' for. Maybe then the grumble will die.

'Work out' so that, you see, we may become—not blameless and pure in the sense of perfect—but children of God who people can actually trust because we're genuine and we're real. And may I also point out that when it says 'children of God without fault', that's the old word for the lamb that was offered without blemish. It's a sacrificial word. You and I offering ourselves to the Lord should live lives that work out our salvation.

Speak out (verses 16–18)

Alec Motyer wrote a lovely commentary on Philippians called *The Richness of Christ* to which I am indebted in various ways. He says this about speaking: 'Lip without life is idle gossip, life without lip is an uninterpreted parable.'

Like all Alec Motyer's statements it contains much for you to think through. He is saying that if you're always talking about things but the way you live denies them, shut up: you're causing more harm than good. But the second half is true for more of us, I believe. We do seek to live a Christian life, we do seek to work it out, but we say 'I'm not the talking sort. I don't say anything about my faith, I just keep it to myself. I try to show it by the way I live.'

'An uninterpreted parable'—what does that mean? If you live a good life by the grace of God, you don't speak about your faith, and nobody knows you're a Christian, who will get the glory? You? 'What a nice person she is, what a good fellow, what an attractive young lady'—but what they need to know, surely, is that it's Jesus who's done it. We're not like that by nature, it's only God's grace. We need to speak out, so the parable may be understood.

I find verse 16 very touching: 'I want to look forward to the day to prove that I've never run in vain—that it's not been empty, my service.'

Now, what do you make of that? Did Paul ever really believe, after all that he'd done, that his service could be empty? I like that lovely human touch. Paul was never falsely humble.

You've met people who say to you, 'I'm really no good and I have nothing to offer.' It's amazing what it does to them if you agree with them. They begin to say, 'Well, I'm not as bad as all *that*...' False humility is worse than pride. And Paul was not falsely humble. He really was anxious that on that great day it would prove that he hadn't run in vain. He was never complacent.

Billy Graham once said that every time he took a mission he took it as if it was his first and as if it was his last. He didn't depend upon the past and say, 'Well, I've been all over the world preaching, I can just do it.' And he didn't assume that he would preach any more afterwards.

Friends, ask God to give you that kind of spirit. Not complacent, not falsely humble, but longing that each day you might not run in vain, longing that as you seek to speak out and work out, others may come to faith through your ministry.

One last comment. Will you note in verse 16: 'As you hold out the word of life.' The verb can mean two things. It can mean what it seems to mean, that is, 'that you may speak out'. Or it can mean that you hold on to the word of life.

May I say, friends, I want you to have both. Holding out the word of life is evangelism, holding on to the word of life is evangelicalism and I am unashamedly an evangelical. That doesn't mean to say that I believe we've got the monopoly of truth and that we've nothing more to learn. But I long that all people should be both evangelistic and evangelical.

I meet some people who are keen to be evangelistic and they're very keen to reach out and to bring people to church, but they've really got no message to offer. I meet some people who are evangelical, but they seem to have no concern for the lost any more. If you and I believe these things, if we have got the word of life, hold it out.

God may be asking you this week to do something new. Take it out and hold on to it. Please don't be ashamed of being evangelical. The word gets a bit of a bad press sometimes. I know we make many mistakes, but I am thankful that I belong to those who hold on to the word of life—and do remember, you and I inherit a precious heritage. If we don't hold on to it and make sure the next generation receives it, whatever denomination you are, however orthodox you may seem to be, an age may come when they've nothing to hold out because you haven't held on.

God, give us grace to hold on and to hold out.

So keep working, keep speaking, keep serving.

3. A Servant's Pilgrimage (Philippians 2:19–3:12)

All preachers have bees that buzz in their bonnet. And the bee that buzzes in my bonnet is 'balanced biblical Christianity' (that's a lot of 'b's that buzz!). I am concerned that Christians should not only expound and study Scripture, but that they should keep the balance of Scripture. If you just pick out texts and preach what you like, then you can make the Bible mean anything—and, what is even worse, you can exaggerate certain truths.

And the lovely thing about this letter to the Philippians is that you get the balance. There was that tremendous picture of the greatness of our Lord, and that great doctrinal passage lifting us to the heavens—and now in the same letter, moving on just a few verses, a very homely touch, in the portrait of Timothy and Epaphroditus. And yet they're all linked together. The Bible takes us to the heights and brings us down to earth, but the down-to-earth is linked to the heights.

Have you noticed? You see, the great thing about Timothy, for example (verse 20), is that he 'takes a genuine interest in your welfare' and he's so different from those who look after their own interests. They were the exact opposite of Jesus, and Timothy was copying Jesus;

and we'll see in Paul's tremendous testimony that he too was echoing Jesus, so the two go very close together.

We were reminded in our first Reading that Jesus, and His humiliation, is the example we are to follow. Peter says that 'Christ suffered for you, leaving you an example' (1 Pet 2:21).

The language recalls how writing was taught in the old Greek world. The letters were written out in perfect script, and the scholar had to copy them underneath. The same method was used not so long ago in British schools.

We have seen that perfect example in Jesus, and what we're going to see this morning is various people—Timothy and Epaphroditus, Paul himself, the Philippian Christians—following the pattern of Jesus and being servants.

Firstly,

A Servant's Pilgrimage

Ministers of Christ
Just before we get into these verses in depth, let me point you to three verses in Colossians 1 where the word 'servant' comes. It's actually a different word from 'slave', it's *diakonos*, the servant, the minister. And will you notice how beautifully it is brought in?

In verse 7 Epaphras is described as 'a minister of Christ'. In verse 23, Paul speaks of himself as 'a servant' of the gospel—it's the same word as 'minister' in the Greek. And in verse 25 he describes himself as a servant of the church. And that's how the order should be. We serve Christ, we serve the gospel, we serve the church.

And I do love the word 'minister'. We Anglican clergy get called all sorts of things. My high church friends call me 'Father', and since I've got two children I bow to that title! My evangelical friends call me 'Brother', and that's tremendous. And those who come to church once a year call me 'Padre'. Well, I'll accept even that. But I love being called 'minister'. For a minister is what I supremely am. We're all servants.

Pen portraits (2: 19–30)

So back to Philippians 2, where we've got these pen portraits of Timothy and Epaphroditus, and then a marvellous personal profile as Paul gives his testimony early in chapter 3—the perfect example of the value of a testimony.

Testimonies can be very dangerous. They can be very self-glorifying things and, let's be honest, they're not always as honest as they should be. A testimony only means anything if it's 'warts and all'; the moment you take the warts out you make it useless. But a testimony is glorifying to Jesus, and Paul, quite naturally, undergirds his teaching with his own experience. And what a wonderful thing that is.

So we're going to look at the pen portraits of Timothy and Epaphroditus, and then we're going to look at a personal profile of Paul.

Verses 19 to 30: there are three people here, two obvious, one not so obvious.

First of all,

A person to be trusted

Timothy was always ready to be a messenger. I sometimes feel sorry for him—Paul was always sending him here, there and everywhere. In verse 19, he sends him on to get news of the Philippians. Timothy wasn't an identi-kit of the travelling jet-set preacher. He was very different. Let me paraphrase 1 Corinthians 16:10, where Paul says to the Corinthians, 'Please, please don't make him afraid; he's a timid character and he finds it hard.' In 1 Timothy 4:12, Paul talks about his youth that must not be despised. In 2 Timothy 1:4, he talks about Timothy's tears; he was an emotional, timid man. And yet, you see, he was always ready, always available.

I'm no Timothy, but I travel quite a bit; and I hate travelling, I really do. I sometimes say to the Lord, 'Why do You call me to travel?' And it's always worse when people say, 'You do enjoy travelling around the world, don't you?' The answer is 'No, I don't, but I do it for the sake of the gospel.' Timothy was always ready. Are you? Most of the time he was only preparing the way for the greater man to come, but he was always ready, always available.

'I have no-one else like him,' says Paul. 'He takes a genuine interest in your welfare.' The Greek word says that he's genuinely anxious, and the word 'genuinely' means it's his birthmark. He's a born-again child of God, and the birthmark of a born-again child of God is that he or she cares more for others than for self.

Have you got that birthmark? Would people say about you or me, that we've got a genuine interest in others? Or would we in honesty have to acknowledge the awful indictment of verse 21: 'Everyone else looks out for his own interests, not those of Jesus Christ'? What an indictment! Timothy stood out. His concern was care for others.

These are very practical matters in Philippians. In your church, and in your discussions, and in your plans, are you thinking about what you get out of it, or how they're treating you? Or is there genuine interest in the welfare of others?

The great testimony of verse 22 is more than the testimony of a man who has led somebody to Christ. There was a link of father and son. And here was a man, verse 22, who has 'slaved with me in the work of the gospel'.

Timothy, a person to be trusted, ready for anything, thinking always of others, genuinely caring for them and ready to work. I hope that's you.

A person to be honoured

Epaphroditus (verse 29) was a person to be honoured.

There must be thousands of people in this country who serve others, and nobody ever thinks of them for the Honours List. But verse 29 emphasises that the honour that matters is the honour that comes from God. I love the phrase 'Honour men like him'.

Do you remember Jim Graham's address last night about the 'anybodies'?[1] God hasn't chosen the mighty, the important, the well off, the clever. He's chosen ordinary people—and Epaphroditus was one such. Honour men like that! We've got it wrong sometimes, and we follow the example of the world and devise our church Honours List. But sometimes we've got it the wrong way round.

Now, what about Epaphroditus? Well, there are four nouns used of him in verse 25. He was a brother, a worker, a soldier, a messenger. They're great nouns.

He worked well with others, too, as we've already seen, and not every Christian does. I was once speaking about C.T. Studd, telling how wonderful he was, and at the end of the meeting an elderly lady stumped out to the front and said, 'Young man'—as I was, then—'I've worked with C.T. Studd—he was impossible, quite impossible!' And she stormed out. And I believe her; but God used such.

There are glorious individualists whom God can use, who are absolutely impossible. Don't model yourself on them. God uses them, thank God he does. But it's a good job we're not all like that. It was said of the great Irish preacher, W.P. Nicholson, that nobody believed a man could be full of rudeness and the Holy Spirit at the same time till they met W.P. Nicholson. But don't model yourself on him!

The mark of a child of God is that they work with others, brothers, sisters, fellow-workers, fellow-soldiers.

If you are the odd eccentric, well, just watch it! But for most of us, we're called to work with others.

Epaphroditus was sensitive: 'He's distressed because you heard he was ill' (verse 26). Isn't that a lovely little touch? Some people love people to know that we're ill. We make quite sure everybody knows, and we exaggerate our illnesses. But here was a man who was upset because others were upset on account of his illness.

I wonder, was the grave illness Paul talks about in verse 27 caused by Epaphroditus risking his life (verse 30)? I don't know. But I know that the word 'almost died' is, in the Greek, exactly what's said about Jesus way back in verse 8, 'unto death'. Jesus was 'unto death'. Epaphroditus was 'almost unto death'. He was patterning Jesus.

And I know that the verb for 'risk his life' in verse 30 is the same word used in Acts 15:26, and it means gambling. Friends, I do hope we have still, whatever age we are, a sense of adventure. I'm afraid that some of us are so security-conscious about what we do with our money and our lives that we never risk anything.

Some people don't take financial risks. Some stay back when it comes to service. They're worried about their health, they're worried about their future. They're very conscious of the risk. But I want to tell you there are evil people in the world who are risking things to propagate *their* gospel. There are militant Muslims who are prepared to throw their lives away for their gospel. We don't understand them. We think they're profoundly wrong. But you tell me why a creed which does not have the truth in its heart produces martyrs, while those of us who claim to have the truth of the gospel and the passion in our souls are so security-conscious.

It may be I'm getting old—I am!—but I get bothered sometimes that even in the ministry it's easy. I went to a clergy conference, and oh! the excitement with which we discussed the Poll Tax, and whether we ought to pay it. We discussed it for hours. We were more concerned with that than with the appointment of a diocesan evangelist. It simply wasn't regarded as so important.

And my heart bleeds. Is this the kind of clergyman of today? Is this the kind of Christian that's going to turn the world upside down?

A person to be discovered

I find a hidden person in these verses. It's Paul of course; the way Paul talks about Timothy and Epaphroditus tells me a lot about him.

I learn of his humility. 'Timothy has served with me, in the work of the gospel' (verse 22). The young Timothy 'served' with the great Paul. And he had great confidence—Timothy was only half-Jewish, Epaphroditus was Gentile, but Paul was absolutely one with them and he loved them and they meant a great deal to him. And yet he was willing to sacrifice them for the sake of others.

I'm talking to older people now—that is, people my age and older. And I'm talking to my own heart. Have you got to the stage where you have no confidence in the future? 'We don't trust the next generation of ministers. Things aren't what they used to be.'

I think of Alan Redpath, whom I mentioned earlier in these Readings. One of the great joys about him is that even to his dying day he believed that the best was yet to be; in his eighties he saw what God was doing and rejoiced in it. 'Keep going, keep the vision clear,' he urged. 'Don't live in the past.'

And I believe we as people who are getting on in years ought to trust the next generation. We don't trust them enough, sometimes.

Just one other thing about Paul that you can discover.

He was always, in everything, submissive to the Lord. Have you noticed it? 'I hope in the Lord Jesus to send Timothy' (verse 19). 'I am confident in the Lord that I myself will come' (verse 24). All his plans were under that 'God willing' umbrella.

And that all leads to verse 1 of chapter 3 (it's often been pointed out that Paul says 'finally' just half-way through his address. It means nothing at all, except that we are moving towards the appointed goal.)

But it is interesting, isn't it: 'Finally, my brothers, rejoice in the Lord!' He's going back to 2:17–18, where he's been exhorting them to rejoice with him. A man in prison—'Rejoice with me!' It's only in the Lord that we can ultimately rejoice. May I leave it with you to ponder? Where is your joy? If your joy is in fellowship, a great church, wonderful experiences—whatever it might be— then if you're in prison like Paul you've lost it.

The prophet Habakkuk closes his words by affirming that even if God takes away all the things that give him joy, and the vine fails, and everything seems to disappear—'I will rejoice in God my Saviour' (cf. Hab 3:17– 18). That's tremendous! And when you and I have got there, we've found the secret of joy.

We've seen the pen-portraits. Now,

A personal profile (3:1–12)
Let's come to this great testimony. This is, if you like, the meat. And first of all,

The context of the testimony (verses 1–3)
What is remarkable—and here's the balance again!— Paul is talking about rejoicing in the Lord, and then suddenly he says, 'But watch out.'

Some commentators suggest that perhaps at that point he put his letter on one side. You do that sometimes, don't you? You start a letter, and a week later you think of finishing it off. He put it down and heard some news from Philippi that bothered him. And so the tone changes. He really was meaning to finish off, he was saying 'finally'; but now he hears news that bothers him about division, so he puts a bit more in.

That's conjecture. But what we know is that Paul is as honest as he is loving—and the two go together. He can say lovely things about Timothy and Epaphroditus and he means it, but look what he talks about in verse 2: 'Those dogs, those men who do evil, those mutilators of the flesh—Watch out.'

Who are they? They're not highly immoral people. They're not those who are dabbling in the occult and doing dangerous practices. They are people who are preaching what I call 'Jesus-plus'. Oh yes, they believed the gospel, but they also said: 'But it's not enough. It's fine to believe in Jesus, but you need more than that. You must be circumcised. And if you're not circumcised, well—you're not really there.'

Have you met them? They're not like that today, of course. But I've met them. 'Well yes, you may be...but if you've not been confirmed or baptised by immersion or speaking in tongues, you're not really there. You may think you've got salvation, but to really be saved you need...'

Please note what Paul does. He first of all says 'Watch out.' In Acts 20:28 he talks to the Ephesian elders. He says, 'Look out for yourselves and for the flock, for false teachers will come in and people from your own ranks will rise up and they will teach heresy. They'll add Jesus-plus. Watch out!' And he uses very strong language about them.

In verse 3 of our passage he speaks positively. 'We are the real circumcision.' I love Paul's absolute honesty.

Tolerance is a right virtue, in its right place. But lack of confidence or assurance is not the mark of a Christian. I believe one of the greatest needs of our day is the need for the doctrine of assurance. But Paul can say with absolute assurance, 'We are the real circumcision.' (Look at Rom 2:28 some time, where Paul says 'The real circumcision is of the heart, not of the flesh.')

Next Paul gives some marks of genuine Christianity. Verse 3: 'We worship by the Spirit of God...glory in Christ Jesus...put no confidence in the flesh.'

Paul's testimony is that real Christianity, irrespective of denomination and emphasis, includes those who worship in the Spirit. Wasn't it our Lord who debated with the woman at the well about the kind of people God wants to worship Him? It doesn't matter where, it doesn't matter how; it's worship in spirit and in truth.

Barnabas came from Jerusalem and had limited knowledge of worship patterns. But when he went to an absolutely different church in Antioch, we are told that he saw the evidence of the grace of God and 'was glad' (Acts 11:23).

If you go to a church that does things very differently from you, do you find it easy to rejoice and be glad? Or are you so obsessed by the differences that you can't worship? What is it that makes a Spirit-filled church? The way they hold their services—or the worship in spirit and truth?

Secondly, they 'glory in Christ Jesus'. Not in their experience or their denomination, but in Christ. They 'put no confidence in the flesh'. I want to pause on that word 'flesh'. What do you think he means? Well, he's not talking about the grosser sins of the flesh, he's talking about confidence in self. 'Flesh' almost equals 'self'. And Paul would go on to say, 'If anybody could have confidence in the self, I could.'

There's the context of his testimony. Here are Christians being led astray. Here are Christians being given 'Jesus-plus'; and Paul wants to say, 'No, no, no.' And instead of giving them deep academic theology, he gives a moving testimony with deep theology in it.

The content of the testimony (verses 4–12)

Now, the content of the testimony. I want to suggest two points. Firstly,

The testimony of a changed confidence (verses 4–8).
I occasionally take missions in parishes, and speak at the local Rotary Club. I'm told that you aren't allowed to give talks on religion. So there I am, taking a mission in the parish, not permitted to talk about the gospel, and allowed fifteen minutes. How do I talk to them about the gospel?

What I normally say is, 'Well now, what I'm doing this week is I'm taking a mission. If you were to come along to the mission, this is what you would hear.' And one has the feeling that Paul is adopting a similar device here, and by doing so, he is actually highlighting the gospel.

Look at the changed confidence. Verse 7: 'What once was profit I now consider loss.' Verse 8: 'I consider it rubbish that I may gain Christ. What once I thought was merit I now count as useless.' He is talking, you see, about those who have confidence in the flesh. For the flesh in the theological sense of the letters of Paul doesn't mean the worst things but the best things. Man at his best, without Christ. Saul of Tarsus was a good man. By his reckoning he was fine, the world looked at Saul of Tarsus or Nicodemus and said, 'Great!'

Jesus looked at Nicodemus and said, 'You must be born again.' Saul needed turning upside down, for his confidence was in—what? Verse 5: his background; verse 6: his activities. Has it changed?

Jesus said that on the day of judgement many people will say, 'Lord, Lord.' That's the people who have got the words without the actions. And others will say, 'Didn't I do this, that and the other in Your name?' They've got the actions without the faith. And our Lord will say: 'Sorry, I don't know you.'

And here's Paul saying, 'This is what I based my confidence in—in my background, in my attainments. I did once, but I've no more confidence in that. That's gone.' He says it all adds up to nothing. It was once profit (verse 7), and now it's loss.

Do you believe that for yourself?

Ah, but just a moment, before I pass on to my last point. Is there a danger that, as a Christian, you've now started to build your confidence on the flesh again? How many people still imagine, 'Of course I'm a sound Christian. I go to this church, I get involved in those things, I go to the Keswick Convention. I'm basing all my spirituality on the things I do, the people I know; and I become a kind of Pharisee very quickly'?

I shall never forget reading Dr Lloyd-Jones on the Sermon on the Mount. I was very challenged when he reached 'Did I not preach in your name?' Suddenly the Lord was speaking to me. 'Philip Hacking, however many sermons you may have preached'—and even then I'd preached a lot—'and however many people may have responded to your sermons, you do not gain heaven because you preach. You are not one of Mine because you happen to have led people to Christ. It's whether you know Me and I know you that counts.'

And I thank the Lord I did know Him, but I needed to be reminded. That was my confidence.

Isn't that why our Lord ends the greatest sermon of all time with that homely illustration of the two houses, one built on the rock and the other on the sand? And are some of us, who started building on the rock, shifting to the sand? We're building our confidence on things that can disappear—'The church isn't what it used to be; I had confidence in people and they've gone.' Build on the rock!

I come to my last point.

A testimony of challenging concern (verses 9–12).
In these verses there is a lovely balance of satisfaction and dissatisfaction.

Are you a satisfied Christian? Yes and no. Because if you're a complacent Christian, then there's something wrong: but I hope you're satisfied that you're in Christ. Paul is, and it keeps on coming out. He knows Christ (verses 8, 10). Yes, of course he knows Him. He is already found in Him. But he wants something deeper.

What does it mean, to be found in Christ? Look at verse 9. It's the end of self-righteousness, it's the beginning of Christ-righteousness. He has stopped building his life on the foundation of his own righteousness.

How can you judge yourself, how can you decide how well you're doing? What a liberation it is to know that's not what it's all about! It's that salvation which God gives me in Christ by grace, received by faith; and when I receive that, then I am justified, I am accepted, I am found to be in Christ. Right through Scripture, there's this scarlet thread. It starts in Genesis 15:6: 'Abram believed and it was reckoned to him for righteousness.'

Standing some time ago by the Martyrs' Memorial in Oxford and thinking about a sermon I was going to preach the next day, I thought, 'How do I get across to young people today why these men were willing to die for what seems like mere doctrine?' Was it so important, justification by grace through faith? Did it really matter? After all, the other people who were opposing called themselves Christians. Did these people die in vain? Would any of us here today think it reasonable to put our hand in the fire

and have it burnt first, because we'd recanted on justification by faith?

I doubt it. But there'd have been no Keswick if they
hadn't. And there'd have been no Bible in our own language if they hadn't. Don't you see how important it was?
And it's so terribly important in an age when we're all
being urged to be much more tolerant and ecumenical and
gather under the wing all those who call themselves Christians. We're in trouble, friends; we're in trouble.

There are people here today who could talk about
persecution, and I'm only at the kindergarten stage. But I
do know what it is to be called intolerant, because I won't
do certain things. I do know what it is to be called unloving, because I stand against practices the Bible condemns.
I object strongly to practising homosexuals in the ministry
of the Church of England, and I say so. 'That's unloving,
that's intolerant.' But, you see, friends, it isn't. It's very
loving.

And I want, and dare, to say it from this platform—but
I'd say it in any platform: I am unashamedly an evangelical, and I do believe evangelical truth is truth. Let's be
careful; there's a lot more we've got to learn, and there
are many things that evangelicals have fought for that
need to be forgotten. Sometimes we've got it wrong.
Evangelicals aren't always right! But the evangelical truth
of the authority of Scripture is that for which we must fight
and to which we hold on. If we lose that, there will be no
evangelisation.

You see, our critics say the opposite; that we're too
strict. 'Make it easier, broaden, broaden...'

And I find Paul battling. You see, the righteousness
which comes through faith in Christ, that comes from God
and is by faith, is the heart of the gospel. Lose that and
you lose not only the truth, but you lose the cutting edge
of the gospel.

That's Paul's satisfaction. But where is his dissatisfaction? It comes out in his longing, in verses 10 to 12. Yes, he knows Christ; yes, he has found justification by faith; but he's not there yet.

Sometimes evangelicals, by battling for the truth, have seemed to be unnecessarily arrogant. You see, we haven't got there yet. We've got the truth, we've got salvation, but we're still longing: and Paul says, 'I want to know Christ.'

Here's the apostle in prison, having served his Lord so faithfully. But he says, 'I want to know Christ, I want to get to know Him better.' The word 'know' is an intimate personal relationship word. And if you love somebody, if you know them, you want to know them better. And Paul wants to know Christ.

Is it not odd—'the power of his resurrection and the fellowship of his sufferings'? I want to say, 'Paul, you've got it the wrong way round. Start with the sufferings, surely?'

Oh no, he's got it the right way round. For when you come to Christ you know something of the reality of the risen power of Christ: new life in Him. And it's only as you go on in the Christian faith you get to know something of the fellowship of His sufferings.

But can I rejoice with you, that even in the sufferings you're close to Christ? It's not just suffering *for* Christ, it's suffering *with* Christ. 'They rejoiced they were counted worthy to suffer for his name's sake.' And if there's a cross in your life, a real cross, you'll be nearer to Jesus than at any other point in your life. You may learn more about Christ that moment than in any sermon in this Keswick Convention tent.

When Abraham was about to offer his son Isaac on the mountain, we read: 'In the mountain of the Lord, it shall be seen' (Gen 22: 14). That was the moment when Abraham learned more of God than he'd learnt all his life up to that point. He learnt something of the heart of Calvary. He was only a stone's throw from Calvary geographically, and theologically he was only a stone's throw away too. He learned the heart of God who put His knife into His Son, and Abraham could drop the knife.

You see what Paul says: 'I want to get close to Him, even if it means suffering with Him'—and so, verse 11, 'somehow'.

There is no suggestion in verse 11 that Paul has any doubts that he's going to get to the resurrection of the dead. In tomorrow's Reading we shall see that for Paul, it was always 'now and not yet'. Paul had no doubt he was going to get to the resurrection from the dead.

What does the word 'somehow' mean? Well, you see, he doesn't know how he's going to get there. 'I know that I shall meet Jesus, I have no doubts about that. I know I'm going to die, unless the Lord returns before that day. But I've no idea what's going to happen between now and then, and thank God I don't. I don't want to know.' Here's Paul in prison, not depressed, but looking on to the great day.

And so we end on verse 12. 'Not that I've got there— yet. Not that I'm already perfect—yet. But I press on to take hold of that for which Christ took hold of me.'

Just hold it, do you see? It's wonderful to me, that is. Here's the apostle in prison, the prisoner of hope, and here he is saying 'the best is yet to be; I'm pressing on; I'm still straining to the future.'

Here we are gathered, people of all ages; and I care not whether you're nineteen or ninety, verse 12 should still be true of you. If Christ has got hold of you, He's got hold of you for a purpose. Have you found that purpose yet? He grabbed you on your Damascus road and now He asks of you to press on toward the mark. It's a great pilgrimage.

You may not be a Paul, none of us will be. You may not

even be a Timothy or an Epaphroditus—no, you're not! You're you; and I—I can't do anything about it—am I. We're all gloriously different, but all of us can go that same pilgrimage with the same Lord to the same glory.

1. See the address by Jim Graham included on p.181 of this volume.

4. A Servant's Resources
(Philippians 3:13–4:23)

I'm assuming you've all done your homework, and I hope you go back with a great joy in the letter to Philippi.

This particular passage is full of goodies. It's like a Christmas pudding—it's marvellous, it's full of good things—with at least three or four classic verses that we often use. When I sign books I often use Philippians 4:13 or 19; lovely, wonderful verses.

Now, there is a danger. You all know what happens if you have too much Christmas pudding. You can go out with acute indigestion—and I wouldn't wish anybody to leave Keswick with that! Success over spiritual indigestion is to go out in obedience to the word to share it with others; then it'll be rich in you. The Dead Sea is a dead sea because everything goes into it and nothing goes out of it. And if at the end of Keswick you've taken it all in and nothing goes out, there will be problems.

So I'm going to share these goodies.

One last thing about them. Study them in context. It is dangerous to string texts together. However clever you may be, you're in trouble if you do that. It's better see even these temendous goodies in their context.

We see in these verses (3:13–21)—we see Paul still the

prisoner, but Paul who was at heart a pastor and a preacher. And I believe those two things should go together. Pastoring and preaching.

When I was first ordained we had a little simplistic tag: 'a home-going parson makes a church-going people'. I wish it were quite as simple as all that, and it isn't, but there's a lot of truth in it. The truth that is in it is that a man or woman who's in touch with people in a normal pastoral relationship, whether a parson or preacher or neither, is going to be infinitely better in expounding Scripture. You don't just prepare sermons in the study, you prepare them also out on the streets and in the home. And you feel with Paul, as he writes these words, that he is a tremendous pastor.

He deals truthfully and lovingly with some sensitive areas. He exemplifies a phrase he uses elsewhere, in Ephesians, 'truthing it in love', or 'speaking the truth in love'.

Some of you are champions of truth. Don't forget it!— but add a little love to it. Some of you are very loving. Keep it up!—but do add a bit of truth to it. There are some people I know who are so gracious and loving that I could never get a realistic estimate from them about anybody else, because they're too generous—they are rare souls, but they do exist. But truth and love always must go together.

And as we read these verses, as we see the pastoral heart of Paul there in prison going out to these Christians at Philippi, going out to us today, going out with us wherever we go after today, we see a balance of the problems to be faced and the resources—and I've got three resources. I'm going to talk about the prize, the inspiration to go forward; the peace, the encouragement to commend Christ; and the principle, the way to be satisfied.

The prize—an inspiration to go forwards (3:13–21)

It's an inspiration with three commands. First,

Press on (verses 13–16)
There is no instant maturity in Christianity. Paul—the great apostle, who's been through so much for God, who's written such marvellous stuff—still says, 'I'm pressing on. I haven't really got there; I haven't really reached where the Lord means me to reach.' So if that's true of Paul, it's true of you and me.

Please don't expect other people to be instantly mature. Sometimes well-established Christians get very worried about some of these younger Christians. They haven't had your background and they haven't had your years of preparation. So don't expect them to be instantly mature any more than you are.

Paul knows that he must go on pressing on.

Would you please note (in verse 14) about the prize for which he presses on, that it's not the prize of his deserving; it's where God has called him, it's the prize of God's grace. There's nothing wrong with looking forward to the right kind of prize. And the prize that he's looking forward to—it's in 1 Peter 5:4, the crown of glory; 2 Timothy 4:8, the crown of righteousness. If that's the kind of reward you look forward to, don't be ashamed of it. It doesn't promise you rewards in this world necessarily, but all the glory of that prize: 'the prize to which God has called me heavenwards in Christ Jesus'.

Now I've got two things to say about this pressing on towards that prize.

Note the dedication (verse 13): 'One thing I do.'

All preachers have what they call their 'sermon-in-the-pocket'. My 'sermon-in-my-pocket' is the five 'one things' of the New Testament. So if suddenly somebody says to me, 'Philip, have you got a word for us?', it's always the five 'one things' from the New Testament that are there waiting (if you want to know what the other four are, I'll tell you afterwards). This is one of them, and it does come five times in the New Testament: 'one thing'.

'One thing I do,' says Paul. This is absolute dedication. Is it fanaticism? No, fanatics are blinkered and are narrow-minded. No, the 'one thing' of Paul is his absolute dedication, whatever he's doing to keep pressing on as a Christian. He isn't always going to be doing religious things. He isn't always going to be reading religious books, but one thing he's doing, he's pressing toward the mark.

And the second point: 'Forgetting what is behind and straining forward to what lies ahead.'

Should you really forget what lies behind? Surely the Bible says we should be remembering, constantly. You could find lots of verses which say 'remember'. But you've got to have not only a good memory, but a good 'forget-tory'. It's a very good thing, to learn how to forget. I meet some people who never get on in the Christian life because they're always looking over their shoulder. They're always looking to the past—it's a guilt from the past.

I don't want to be simplistic. Some of you have got problems with guilt from the past that you've got to get sorted out. But I am saying that you will never run while you're still living in that guilt, living with that prejudice. Some of you aren't getting anywhere because you still hang on to the prejudices and the problems of the past; and some of us—and some of our churches—don't press on, don't strain forward, because we're looking behind to the successes of the past. We're living on our reputation. So forget what lies behind you. Strain to what lies ahead.

I love the challenge that comes out in verses 15 and 16. What Paul is saying, I think, is (look at verse 16): 'Live up to the truth you now know.' You haven't reached maturity yet. We're always getting more and more mature. You be responsible to respond to the truth you know. You've got a lot more to learn, so have I; but respond to the truth you've learned.

Now, verse 15. Paul could say, 'Look, if you're mature you will agree with me and if you don't agree with me, never mind, one day you will! You'll discover that I am right.' I love that splendid assurance that Paul has. I think he's a right to say it, because he's not only a preacher, he is one of those through whom God chose to give us the inspired word of God.

But what he is saying is, 'Please don't pretend to be more mature than you are.' There are Christians who come to Keswick who think they've nothing to learn. And if they're honest, they're much better at judging the preacher than listening to what the preacher would say. If that's how we come then we need to be changed. I hope at the end of this week we have been learning more, becoming more mature, pressing on. Remember, the Christian race is a marathon and the rest of your life you'll be running. Press on, with a prize ahead.

Watch out (verses 17–19)
An honest pastor will encourage you to press on and will also say, 'I need to warn you.'

Please note (verse 18) that he warns with tears. If you find it easy to warn and rebuke there's something wrong. It hurt Paul to have to do it. You can find, in Acts 20, he says, 'I warned everyone night and day with tears.'

But, you see, if you're a faithful pastor, then you've got to tell your people that there are enemies of the cross of Christ (verse 18). There are those whose teaching denies the efficacy of the cross, and the need for a cross. There are those who would insist we all get to heaven in any case so why bother with the cross? I mean, why did God send

His only Son to die on the cross if in fact we're all going to heaven in any case? What sacrilegious nonsense! They're enemies of the cross of Christ! The fact that they may belong to the same denomination as myself or they call themselves what I call myself makes no difference. They are enemies of the cross.

It's not a matter of two ways of looking at it. Some of the truths of Scripture are so abundantly clear that if you deny the need for the atonement or deny the efficacy of the cross, it's not just another opinion, it's false teaching and it's an enemy of the cross of Christ.

And Paul, because he cares for his people, says about them, 'Look at the difference you see: our end is heaven; their destiny is destruction.'

A solemn word; a real word. There are two roads; and one leads to life and one death.

They in this world worship self and greed. Their god is their stomach. Not just what they eat but the whole self-satisfaction is what they live for, and they actually glory or boast about the things of which they should be ashamed. And they are completely worldly; their mind is on earthly things.

Beware—they existed then; they exist now. They dress up in sheep's clothing. You see, I think Satan's very clever, he loves to distract us. It could well be that this kind of thing is much more dangerous than some of the more obvious satanism and the occult and so on. Oh yes, they are dangerous, but we see them for what they are. That's the devil dressed up as the devil. But when he's dressed up as an angel of light he's much more subtle and while we're chasing the devil dressed up as the devil he's coming in dressed as an angel of light, and we haven't spotted that he's there.

Look up (verses 20–21)

Here's the difference. We have hope. 'Our hope,' says Paul, 'is, our citizenship's in heaven, and we're waiting for our Saviour to come from heaven. We don't belong here. We're just passing through.' And I hope we believe that.

Do you remember the old patriarchs of the Old Testament, Abram, Isaac and Jacob? It says about them—just note the phrase—they pitched their tent and they built their altar. And when they moved on, the tent moved with them and the altar remained. Their spiritual life was real; that was the permanent thing. What was not important was where they lived.

We live in a different world. We can't just pick up our tent and move on. But I wonder if it could be seen to be true in our lives that in fact the real thing about us is our worship, our relationship to God, our altar; and the thing that doesn't matter very much is our possessions. We brought nothing into this world and we take nothing out.

We say we believe it—but we spend our money and our concern and our love on the things of this world. Do you give more to missions in a year than you spend on your holiday in a year? And if you don't, don't you have a conscience about it? You ought to have. I guess many Christians, if they're honest, would have to admit there isn't any relationship between the two. And if I said to the Lord, 'Well, I need a holiday so I'm going to spend £500 on a good holiday this year and I'll give £20 to the mission, but I love You, Lord,' the Lord says, 'You don't, you love yourself, you old hypocrite!'

Which is the tent and which is the altar in your life? We've no abiding city here. We're moving on. Our citizenship's in heaven and we're waiting for a Saviour—that lovely picture in verse 20, at the end—the Lord Jesus Christ with all His titles is going to come back.

I hope you believe that great doctrine of our Lord's

return. We wait for that day and with our Lord's return (verse 21) there's the picture of the resurrection body.

Verse 21 is full of notes of power: three strong words all to do with power, dynamic, energy, strength; and all the power of God will one day make this body like His glorified body. Read 1 Corinthians 15:35 onwards where Paul argues with people who say you can't believe the body's raised. Immortality of the soul? Yes, that's all right. Body raised? Paul says, 'You foolish man.' Every time a seed dies, out of the dead seed comes life, every spring. If God can do it with a seed, He can do it with people made in the image of God. And the body's going to be raised.

But just note two things. It's only then that the body's going to be made perfect (verse 21). The Bible insists that our outward body in this world is aging and decaying. Some of us do our best to hold it back, we try to pretend we're younger than we are, we do all sorts of odd things to hold back the tide of the years. But we're wasting our time, because inevitably that's going to happen and it's only in heaven that our body will be perfect.

The theology here is very important. God does give us health—in His grace and mercy He often brings us healing—but one day that body of yours is going to die. You'll never stop that, ever, ever. And only in heaven...there's a 'not yet' about some truths.

It is not true that we can always expect to be healthy in this life. It is not true it's a mark of your spiritual maturity that you're never ill. Some of the greatest saints I know have suffered enormously. People who want to tell us that if you love the Lord you will always be well are an insult to them and their faith. This body will decay. Then there'll be a glorified body. I look on to that day, and so must you.

And again, if I may say so, isn't it good to look after our bodies on earth? Of course. God means us to use our bodies to His glory. Of course, He wants us to be fit, He wants us to be sensible what we do with our bodies. But I also want to tell you something. The devil would love to say to you, and to me, 'Aha, take it easy, you're doing too much!' Maybe I am, maybe you are, but I want to tell the devil, 'Look I've only got one life to live and I do need to be balanced and wise.'

But the greatest danger for the greater number of people is not that they're doing too much for God but that they're doing too little. Now, again I find it difficult as a preacher. For if I preach 'Roll up your sleeves; do more,' the ones who are doing too much say, 'Right, I'm with you, Vicar.' And if I say, 'Learn to rest in the Lord,' the ones who are resting go fully asleep and they say, 'Thank You, Lord.' Some of you need to rest in the Lord and most of you need to say, 'I've only one life to live and I'll use this body to the full, and if God calls me home early it wouldn't be disaster, would it?' On that day there'll be a glorified body.

We press on, we watch out and we look up. There's the prize that lies ahead. The inspiration to go forward.

I'm not a runner. I have never run in a marathon. Have you? There aren't many of us around who haven't run in marathons—it's the thing to do nowadays! But I am running in the marathon of the Christian life and, by God's grace, I'm going to keep pressing on towards the prize.

The peace—an encouragement to commend Christ (4:1–9)

Have you noticed two phrases that balance each other? 'The peace of God' (4:7) and 'the God of peace' (4:9).

Here are two lovely promises, two great resources. The peace of God, the God of peace. Note the word 'and' before them both: 'and the peace of God'; 'and the God of peace.' The word 'and' links back with what's gone before. If I want to know the peace of God there's something I must do; if I want to know the God of peace there's something I must do.

Let's look then at commending Christ.

In the church (verses 1–3)
Notice how Paul does it.

He's talked at the end of chapter 3 about the glory of heaven and our citizenship being there, and in 4:1 he says, 'And I'm looking forward in that day to seeing you there. I may never see you again in the flesh, some of you, but you're my joy and my crown, my brothers, my beloved, and I want you to stand firm because there's still a way to go, maybe, before that day. The Lord is near [4:5] but we never know the day, we never know the hour, and I long for the day when you are, and will be seen to be, my joy and crown.' It's the same phrase as in 1 Thessalonians 2:19.

I pause just for a second. Those of us who serve the Lord in different ways, who seek to lead others to Jesus— what a joy it will be on that day, that there will be those there who'll be there because we've been faithful. Maybe because we've prayed. We might have said nothing, just prayed. I suppose I also have a gut feeling there might be somebody who could have been there and won't be there because I didn't pray and witness. Now, that's always there to keep me very humble. But Paul will look unto that day of 'my joy and my crown'.

And as he thinks of that day of heaven he then remembers there's trouble in the church and he talks about this strange disagreement between those two ladies, Euodia and Syntyche. Notice carefully how he deals with all this. He's been talking about heaven, but he recognises that on earth it isn't quite like that; and there's a disagreement going on between these two ladies. Learn from him as he handles the situation.

First he asks them to agree: and he suggests to them (verse 3) that they've helped him, 'They've contended at my side.'

How sad when people who have served with you are now at loggerheads with each other. How sad that those who are going to be together in heaven, whose names are in the Book of Life, can't meet on earth. Are there people who take the communion with you, with whom you're in disagreement? Isn't there something in the Bible and the prayer book about being in love and charity with your neighbours? And Paul is simply saying, 'Look, you've worked with me, your name's in the Book of Life, get right.'

But then he's very wise. He talks to somebody else called 'loyal yoke-fellow'; we don't know who he is, but somebody who has also served with them, and says, 'Go on—help them, help to restore them. Restore them'—as he says in Galatians 6—'in a spirit of penitence.'

What a marvellous ministry it is to restore. Are you the kind of Christian who helps to bring people together in the Lord?

What were Euodia and Syntyche arguing about? Wouldn't you like to know? We don't know and Paul in his wisdom doesn't tell us. It doesn't matter. In a sense this is going to cover every disagreement there ever has been in the church. Oh I've no doubt it could well have had some sort of doctrinal overtones, but it probably was just a personal matter when it came down to the pinch. But we don't know, and Paul in his wisdom doesn't go on about the issue. He doesn't make the issue bigger than it is.

You know, sometimes we blow things up out of all proportion, and what starts as being something fairly unimportant, and could easily be sorted out, gets bigger and bigger and bigger because we make it bigger. Paul's very wise, and he believes that in the church there can be peace, reconciliation.

In the Christian (verses 4–9)

You see, the public problems of the church require the private solutions of individuals, and he's talked to the individuals and now he says, 'All right, rejoice in the Lord always.'

He brings them back to their relationship in the Lord, and says, 'Rejoice all the time. And again I say, rejoice.'

I told you it's from prison and it's a letter full of joy— sixteen times in 104 verses—but it's not glib joy. The rejoicing that Paul is talking about is rejoicing in the Lord *in* every circumstance—not *at* every circumstance. You don't rejoice because you're ill, but you can rejoice in your illness at the presence of God. That's a very different thing.

And alongside rejoicing—just note the phrase (verse 5a) 'Let your gentleness be evident.'

Oh for that blend of enthusiasm and gentleness! I pray it for myself. I won't tell you which I think I've got more than the other—you might have guessed—but I pray that all of us might be enthusiastic and gentle.

And the challenge is, 'The Lord is near.' He's coming back again—or He's near because He's always around us—either; both.

And in the Christian there needs to be this joy and this gentleness with the awareness that we may discover (in verse 7) the peace of God, which transcends all understanding.

The peace of God is not a feeling inside, it's got nothing to do with being placid, it's everything to do with being at 'peace with God through our Lord Jesus Christ' (Rom 5:1); 'My peace I give to you' (Jn 14:27). And that kind of peace is utterly supernatural.

I'm sure there are many people here who could give

their testimony today about how in the midst of everything going wrong around them, they discovered the peace of God which passes all understanding.

But can I tell you how you may know it? Verse 6: 'Don't be anxious but in everything by prayer and petition, with thanksgiving bring your requests. And the peace of God...' Do you know, if you learn to say 'thank You' to God in every circumstance, then you will learn the peace of God in every circumstance; but if you are rebellious and grumbling in your circumstances, you'll never know the peace of God. With thanksgiving bring your requests and you will discover the peace of God in your heart. Note the verb in verse 7: 'guard'—it means to garrison, as if a protective army were surrounding your heart.

Before we get to know the God of peace, Paul asks us to use our mind. 'Whatever is true, whatever is noble.'

I was once at a school where they liked to read bits of the Bible which weren't 'doctrinal'. This passage was thought to be rather nice; you could read it without being 'doctrinal'. 'Whatever is noble, whatever is true, whatever is lovely...'

But they were wrong! It's extremely doctrinal. What Paul is saying is, 'Put your mind to work on things which are good—and things which are good are found in a God who is good, in the word of God which is good, in Christian people who are good, whatever, whatever, whatever.'

An old Puritan had a quaint saying, 'You can't stop a bird landing on your head, but you can stop it building a nest there.' Now, you can ponder that profound statement. What it means is, 'You cannot stop an evil, impure, wrong thought entering your mind, but you can stop cherishing it.' That's the nest.

I shall never forget hearing Dr Martyn Lloyd-Jones thundering home a message at the time of the Profumo scandal. I remember him saying, 'There were many people who read the paper, read all about these awful immoral things happening...and they loved every minute of reading it. And,' he said, 'thousands of people have committed adultery by proxy.' And I listened to that because I used to read all about it.

Do you read all those things in the paper and say, 'Well, I'm reading it because I ought to know what's going on, and aren't they terrible people, aren't they evil people!'? And God is our witness—deep down in our hearts we enjoy it. It feeds something in us. And even while we say, 'What terrible people!' there's a bit of us that loves it.

But it's not just to do with sexual immorality. I believe you and I have got to learn by the grace of God to use our minds to think of things that are good. Yes, to feed them with the word of God.

Do buy Christian books. A lot of Christians never read anything—and it isn't true you haven't got time. That's nonsense! I'm not saying you should be reading Christian books all the time. But I find it strange that with the thousands of people at Keswick, comparatively few books are bought. I would have expected at least everybody to buy at least one book before they went back from Keswick—and more—so you can feed your mind with things that are good, with tapes that help you, because it seems to me that's what Paul's saying.

And he goes further (verse 9): Not only think of things that are good, but also 'Whatever you've learned or received or heard, do.' And these Bible Readings of mine, whatever merit they may have had or none, will be useless unless they lead to some action in the lives of some people. My prayer is that by God's grace, they will. Whatever you've seen or learned or received, do—and the value of Keswick will be seen not in what we feel like here, but in what happens hereafter.

You know, sometimes we go to Christian meetings and the atmosphere is electric and people say it was marvellous—but it hasn't made a scrap of difference to the way people live. It was just to do with the meeting. I love there to be a feel about a meeting. But I do long to know, not that there's a feeling, but that it leads to action. 'Whatever you have...do.'

Then, says verse 9, 'And the God of peace will be with you.' If you want the God of peace to be with you—and that's more wonderful than the peace of God; you've got God Himself with you then if you want it—keep your mind on things that are good, obey what you hear—and the God of peace will be with you.

Since you all want to do some homework—you won't know what to do with yourself after these Bible Readings are finished!—may I just suggest to you, there are three times at least where the phrase 'the God of peace' comes in the New Testament. And it's interesting to me—I'm not going to tell you where they are, you can find them— 'the God of peace'. I'll give you a clue and then you can find them.

The God of peace, as I see it in Scripture, is always to do with dynamic things. 'The God of peace who brought again from the dead our Lord Jesus'—everybody's writing down Hebrews 13:20—you all knew that verse, didn't you! And 'The God of peace will sanctify you wholly' (1 Thess 5:23); 'The God of peace will shortly crush Satan under your feet' (Rom 16:20). Isn't it strange? They're all dynamic concepts! The God of peace is going to bring Jesus from the dead and transform you. The God of peace will destroy Satan under your feet. The God of peace will sanctify you wholly. The God of peace will be with you.

It's not God saying, 'Go out with Me and you're going

to have a lovely peaceful, placid time.' He's saying, 'Trust Me and life will never be the same again.' And I want it, and I hope you do.

Finally, then,

The principle, the way to be satisfied (4:10–23)

Two things. First of all,

The secret of contentment

I said it the first morning; it's a thank-you letter. And these verses are thank-you's.

Again, I love Paul's back-handed thanks in verse 11. He said, 'I'm thanking you for your concern. I could have managed without it but thank you very much.' It's a nice way of putting it. But what he is saying is, 'Yes, it's meant a lot to me that you've given me that gift, but I have learnt [note the phrase in verse 12]—I've learnt the secret of being content in any and every situation.'

Have you? Content in *every* situation? Tough, isn't it. I'm still learning. But Paul is saying, 'I've learnt the secret.' It's not some mystical secret. It's not like the Stoics who'd learnt to grit their teeth, whatever. It was something much deeper. He'd learnt to prove the Lord.

Thank God, when God pours things richly upon you spiritually. If you're feeling on the top of a wave today—I hope you are—thank God! But then, when you are thrown up against difficult circumstances, have you learnt in them to be content? And if by God's grace you are doing well financially, well thank God, but use it well, sacrificially. If you're battling, if life is very insecure, thank God because you'll learn some lessons. Proverbs 30:8–9: 'Give me neither poverty nor riches but give me only my daily bread. Otherwise I may have too much and disown you and say, 'Who is the Lord?' Or I may become poor and steal, and so dishonour the name of my God.'

Will you pray that? 'Give me neither poverty nor riches'—but whatever, the secret of contentment.

Then secondly, and finally,

The source of contentment

Two sources, in fact. One, of course, is these Philippian Christians. In verses 14–18, he thanks them that they've been giving generously.

Remember the New Testament principle that we who are blessed must share with those who aren't. In your city, in the world, in your church. You see the principle, if God's blessed you then you share with others. Wasn't it John Wesley who learnt to live off very little, so that when he got more and more as he went on in life, he didn't spend more and more on himself? He only spent the same on himself as he did at the beginning of his life, and the rest he gave away.

Have we got anywhere near that? 'My standard of living must go on improving.' Why? We always assume it must, that we must not allow our standard of living to go down. But I'm not sure why we shouldn't necessarily, if by 'standard of living' you mean being able to live at ease and comfort. And so the biblical principle is that those who have, share with others; and Paul is not ashamed to accept what these people have given him.

But the principal source of his contentment comes in those two great verses, 13 and 19. Just hold them together: 'I can do everything through him who gives me strength' and 'My God will meet all your needs according to his glorious riches in Christ Jesus.' They say almost the same thing. Here is Paul—all things—every need—in Jesus—my God—and he says to these Christians, 'If you give and share with others, don't worry.'

There are many of us who expect that God will supply 'all our luxuries' and if so be there are millions of people dying of starvation, 'I'll give them £10 a year as a gift. Just what it costs me to have a meal in a good restaurant. For an evening meal, that's what I'll give for a year to feed the millions.' God, help us to be honest!

All our needs—'According to his riches in glory by Christ Jesus.'

Our Lord doesn't give out of His riches. If a millionaire put £5 in a collection plate it would be *out* of his riches, but it wouldn't be *according* to his riches. He wouldn't even know it had gone. But our Lord's supply is endless. And that's why you have the great doxology 'To God and Father be glory for ever and ever, Amen.' A great God.

In the last few verses, Paul brings greetings to all the saints in Philippi and he brings them, please note (verse 22) from those who belong to Caesar's household. Now, that could well have included—we're only guessing now—some of those soldiers, the Praetorian Guard, the crack regiment, the people who'd been near Paul in Rome. And if that's so, what a lovely thought that here were some people who had come to Christ through Paul's imprisonment who had never been to Philippi, who didn't know a single one of them, but sent greetings.

I want to finish with a personal illustration. I was taking a mission recently, and a young man gave his testimony. He had become a Christian in prison—that's the link with this letter. He was one of those who was involved in the Heisel Stadium riot in Belgium. I never did discover exactly what he did, but he admitted the fact that he had caused trouble and he accepted the fact that he was suffering, in that sense, rightly for what he did. And he gave a lovely testimony. Afterwards, hearing that I was a football supporter, he said, as he was a Liverpool supporter and I am a Sheffield Wednesday supporter, 'Were you there at that match two years ago, when Sheffield Wednesday beat us at Anfield?'

Now, the number of times Sheffield Wednesday win at Anfield is so rare, of course I could not forget that occasion, and I had been present at that match. And he said, 'Do you know, if I'd met you coming out of the ground that day when you beat us, I would have gladly slit your throat! And now,' he said, 'we're standing on the same platform speaking about Jesus.'

Isn't it a funny world? I pondered this extraordinary piece of the Providence of God. I throw it out to you because I want to suggest to you that there's a God of great grace working in the world who could change a lad like that.

And I'll tell you something too. I am no less a product of amazing grace than that young fellow who was converted in prison—and a young convert with a lovely Liverpool accent and a man who's been preaching for more years than he cares to remember both stood simply to testify to the grace of the Lord Jesus.

I pointed out when we began that this letter begins and ends with grace. And my prayer is that the grace of God will enable us, each one, to be servants, prisoners of hope in a world that needs to know there is freedom. His service is perfect freedom.

Studies in Ephesians

by Rev. Chuck Smith

1. His Grace and Peace (Ephesians 1:1–2)

About the turn of this millenium, the city of Ephesus was one of the major trade centres of the world. Most of the goods that came from the east to the metropolis of Rome came through the city of Ephesus.

Paul talks in the first chapter of our being sealed with 'that Holy Spirit of promise' (verse 13). The merchants from Rome would go to the city of Ephesus, where they would purchase merchandise that they wanted to sell in their shops in Rome. Having made their purchases, they would place their wax seal of ownership upon that merchandise. Then it would be carried by ship and land and ship again to Puteoli. When it arrived at the sea-port of Puteoli, the merchants would go down and inspect the merchandise, looking for that seal of ownership by which they could claim their goods.

To this busy trade centre of Ephesus, in the Jewish synagogue one morning, there came a man by the name of Apollos, who was mighty in the Scriptures and able to prove by the Scriptures that Jesus was the Messiah. Many of the Jews believed in Jesus at the preaching of Apollos (cf. Acts 18:24–28).

However, there was already there in the synagogue a

couple who had come from Corinth, whose names were Aquila and Priscilla. They had been tent-makers in Corinth and there they had become acquainted with Paul the apostle. And when Apollos came and was so mighty in the Scriptures, they took him aside and explained the word of God a little more thoroughly to him, because at the beginning all he knew was the baptism of John, and, no doubt, the witness of John concerning Jesus Christ: that He was the Lamb of God who takes away the sin of the world.

Apollos moved from Ephesus to Corinth, and from Macedonia there came Paul the apostle to the church in Ephesus. And as he came to the church, he evidently saw that there was something missing in their Christian experience—perhaps a lack of vitality or excitement about the Lord.

And so as he was trying to discern just what was missing in this church of Ephesus, he asked them the question, 'Did you receive the Holy Spirit when you believed, or since you believed?'

They said, 'We haven't even heard of the Holy Spirit.'

He said, 'Well, my! How then were you baptised?'—because Jesus said, 'Baptising them in the name of the Father, and of the Son, and of the Holy Spirit...' (Mt 28:19). 'How were you then baptised?'

And they said, 'John's baptism.'

So Paul went on to explain a little more fully. And then as he laid his hands upon them they received the Holy Spirit. Paul remained there for six months in the synagogue ministering to them, until he was finally kicked out. Then he went to the school of Tyrannus, where for two more years he continued to teach and establish the church in Ephesus.

So, after the two-and-a-half years, we read that the gospel spread throughout all of Asia—that is, that portion of Asia. Ephesus was the centre of the revival that spread to Colosse, to Galatia, to Pergamos, to Thyatira, to Laodicea. Throughout that area the gospel spread through the two-and-a-half-year ministry of Paul there in Ephesus.

And now, Paul, in about the year AD 64, is a house-prisoner in Rome.

Sometimes we wonder why God allows us periods when we cannot be as active as we once were in the ministry, or in our service to Him; but we know that all things work together for good to those who love God. And if it had not been for Paul's imprisonment in Rome, it is quite possible that we would be without the tremendous assistance of the epistles that were written while he was in prison in Rome.

Had Paul been free and been travelling, he probably would have just gone to Ephesus, to Philippi, to Colossae, and would have ministered personally to them. Being restricted by chains in Rome, he had to write to them. But the result—thank God!—is these glorious prison epistles, that have set for us a steadfastness of doctrine within the church.

And one of those epistles that Paul wrote was to the church at Ephesus.

It is thought that this letter was also sent to the church of Laodicea. In some of the older manuscripts, the words 'at Ephesus' in verse 1 are omitted, so that the address would read, 'To the saints and to the faithful in Christ Jesus.' At the same time Paul wrote his epistle to Colosse and perhaps the Philemon epistle; they were carried by Tychicus to these areas with personal greetings from Paul. In his letter to the Colossians, he referred to the letter to the Laodiceans. 'When you've read this, then get the letter that I wrote to them and read it also.'

So it is thought that this letter to the Ephesians is actually a general letter to the church. Surely we qualify!

Paul wrote to the saints and the faithful in Christ Jesus, wherever you are and whoever you are.

So, with that as background, let's begin our study of the book of Ephesians.

The salutation (1:1–2)

The author—Paul the apostle (verse 1)
The word 'apostle' means 'one who has been sent out'.

In the early church, the requirements for apostleship were, number one, a person who had companied Christ from the beginning, who could bear eye-witness to the resurrection of Jesus Christ.

You will remember that as the disciples were assembling together after the resurrection and ascension of Jesus, Peter stood up in their midst and said, 'Brothers, it's necessary that we choose someone to take the place of Judas Iscariot.' And then he quoted a couple of psalms that are not placed together in the book of Psalms; but Peter relates them together to argue that it was necessary that they choose someone to take the bishopric of Judas, who by transgression fell.

So they appointed two—Matthias and Barsabas. And they prayed and cast lots to determine which of the two would be chosen as an apostle. The lot fell upon Matthias, as we know. Peter's criterion was: 'We need someone who has companied with us from the beginning who can bear eye-witness to the resurrection.'

I have some questions in my mind about this matter of man making a choice. I think that there are several things here that could be challenged.

Firstly, the discerning of the will of God by casting lots. That is how the soldiers sought to discern who should get the robe of Jesus. It was a gamble, to determine which direction to go.

However, it's believed that in the New Testament, the

'lot' of verse 26 was probably a copy of the Urim and Thummim of the Old Testament that the priest used to discern the will of God; so there was a New Testament adaptation of the process.

But there's another problem that I have, and I think it's a problem that we often create when we come to the Lord.

They chose two, and then they said, 'Lord, which of these two do You want?' I think that oftentimes we limit God by choosing two. Maybe God has someone else in mind who is not on our list, and we give God only two choices. It's important that when we come to God we should leave the door wide open and say, 'Lord, what do You want?', rather than limit His choice to two.

I wonder, could Matthias ever say: 'Matthias, an apostle of Jesus Christ by the will of God'? Or was it just by a chance casting of the lot? And did God have anything to do with it?

There are many questions today concerning ordination. But I am convinced that man cannot ordain anybody for the ministry. I believe that only God can do that, and at best man can only ratify what God has done. And I believe that man has laid hands on many men to ordain them for the ministry, whom God has not ordained; and there are many men on whom men have never laid hands, who have been ordained by God for the ministry.

Let me say that if I had my choice, I would take the ordination from God!

'Are all apostles?' asks Paul in 1 Corinthians 12:29ff. 'Are all prophets? are all teachers? are all workers of miracles? have all the gifts of healing?'

We know that the rhetorical questions bring forth the answer 'No'. God has appointed some, but not all are called to be an apostle.

There was another requirement for apostleship in the

biblical days. It seems that it was necessary to have the gift of working miracles in his life. Paul writes to the Galatian church and defends his title as an apostle: 'Have I not seen the risen Christ?' (that's one of the requirements), and 'Are not the works of an apostle wrought by me?' (referring to the miracles that were wrought through Paul).

In this sense I am not certain that there are apostles today within the church. Now, I know that there are certain groups that have established apostleships. I know that the Mormons claim to be the only true church because they declare that they are the only church today that has twelve apostles governing the church. And in some Charismatic circles in the United States today there are those who have taken the title of apostle. Usually it is in the context of a shepherding group; they take the title of an apostle so that they can speak with apostolic authority and give people the directions for their lives. A lot of damage has come out of that shepherding movement and, thank God, it's all but dead in the United States now, having done its damage.

So I have serious questions in my mind concerning apostleship. I am not certain that there are any apostles today in the biblical sense.

But I am sure that the other ministry gifts continue— evangelists, prophets, pastor-teachers and so on. I don't think that anyone can question the fact that Billy Graham is a prophet of God in these days almost to the whole world. I don't think you can deny his prophetic office. God has given him the ear of the kings and leaders of the world, and like Jeremiah and Isaiah he stands up to proclaim the importance of our turning to God completely and fully if we're going to survive. And I thank God for this man of God and for his prophetic ministry.

For myself, I would have to say, 'Chuck, a pastor-teacher by the will of God.' One of the most difficult things in the world is to try to be something that you're not 'by the will of God'. For many years I sought to be Chuck the evangelist. But I could not add 'by the will of God'. It was by the will of my denomination, because the denomination that I served was primarily an evangelistic association. Thus all my sermons were evangelistic sermons. They all had an evangelistic appeal. There was always raising of hands, the coming forward, the invitation given at the end of each sermon—because the first thing I had to report on my denominational report was how many people were saved this past month. And there was always, then, that pressure to be able to put numbers in that box, so that when the bishop looked over the reports he would say, 'Oh yes, here's a young man who's doing well. Look how many conversions there are.'

And so there was pressure to be Chuck the evangelist.

But I discovered that one of the most frustrating things was to have a powerful evangelistic sermon burning in your heart. Sometimes the Lord would give me a sermon that was so powerful I was convinced that it would convince the hardest sinner to accept Jesus Christ. 'No sinner could sit through this message without receiving the Lord. This is dynamite!' And I would go to church with my heart burning, hardly able to wait to get in the pulpit and deliver my soul of this powerful evangelistic message. But when I looked at the congregation, there wouldn't be a sinner in the house!

That's frustrating. To have a dynamic evangelistic sermon, and not a sinner to preach it to! So all through the hymns you're praying, 'God, send in at least one sinner, please!' It was too late to conjure up another sermon. You had to go ahead and preach that evangelistic sermon, knowing that there were no sinners to receive Christ.

But, of course, you could always add a few little addendums to your message. 'If you folks were only serving the

Lord as you ought to be serving the Lord, there would be sinners in this place tonight. You would have brought your neighbours! You're failing God! You're not being the witness you should be!' And I'd take it out on the saints that were there, because I was frustrated trying to be Chuck the evangelist.

My dear wife sought to help me. She said, 'Honey, you're not dynamic enough. Watch Billy Graham! He doesn't just stand behind the pulpit, he moves around. You've got to be more dynamic. You've got to start moving around.' So I began to watch Billy Graham. And I decided one Sunday morning I was going to be dynamic like him. I was coming to the main point of my message. I grabbed the microphone, marched over to the edge of the platform, I raised my finger ready to press home a powerful point—all just like Billy Graham—when my mind went blank!

The only thing I could think was, 'How foolish I must look/ over here, with nothing to say.' I couldn't even remember my text. I stood there for a moment in silence, and then let my finger drop, put the microphone back in its place, and looked at my notes. But it was over. That was my last endeavour to be dynamic. I realised I'm not Chuck the evangelist, and I never was Chuck the evangelist 'by the will of God'.

You know, many times people are trying to fulfil ministries to which God has not called them. The Bible tells us to make our calling and election sure. Often a person is doing what they are doing because there's been pressure put upon them to do it: 'Here, we don't have a Sunday school teacher for our high school age-group—would you teach them?' But maybe you're not called by God to it. And so we can be trying to fulfil a ministry to which God has not called us, ordained us or anointed us. That's the toughest thing in the world: to try to be something that God has not made you.

So the question is, 'What are *you*, by the will of God?' If you substitute your own name for Paul's, can you tell what you are, by the will of God? Do you know what place God has called you to fulfil in life, in the body of Christ?

We are told: 'Make your calling and election sure.' But do you really know what your calling is, what God's will for your life is? This is of primary importance to every one of us. If you can't say, 'John, Mary'—or whatever your name may be—'by the will of God', then I pray that before this Convention is over, God's Spirit will work in such a way that you'll find God's direction for your life.

Why? Because I would like to suggest that God has you here on the earth for one purpose, and that's to fulfil His will. How can you fulfil His will, if you don't know what His will is for you?

In Revelation 4:11, as the elders are responding to the praise of the cherubim before the throne of God, they declare, 'Thou art worthy, O Lord, to receive glory and honour and power: for thou hast created all things, and for thy pleasure they are and were created.' Mark that down: you're part of all creation, and you were created for God's good pleasure.

You say, 'I don't like that. I don't think that it's fair that God should just create me for His pleasure. I'm going to live for my own pleasure. I'm going to do my own thing.' And there are many who rebel against this truth, that they were created for God's good pleasure.

Well, like it or not, that's the way it is. And I can assure you, if you seek to live in such a way as to please God, you will find your life will be rich, it will be full, it will be like an overflowing cup. But if you live to please yourself your life will end up empty, filled with frustration. You will be

like Solomon, who did so many things to please himself—
building great monuments, amassing wealth, and gaining
of all understanding—and he finally said, 'Emptiness,
emptiness. Everything is empty and frustrating.'

But you'll find that in pleasing God you please yourself.
He has written His law in the fleshly tablets of your heart,
and He writes His good pleasure right on your heart, so
that you can say with Jesus, 'I delight to do Thy will, O
Lord. It's the joy of my life. It's the delight of my life.'

God has blessed us by His grace so abundantly; and
because of these tremendous blessings that God has
bestowed upon us, my one son often says, 'Dad, why do
you go at it so hard? Why do you keep pushing so hard?
You could retire, you could spend the rest of your life
writing or doing whatever you want. Why do you push so
hard? Why do you just keep going, Dad? Why don't you
retire?' (I think he thinks, '... And let me take over'!)

And I say, 'Son, if I would retire, what would I do for
fun?' I enjoy so much what I'm doing. It's my joy, it's my
plesure, it's my delight—pleasing Him brings such fulfilment, such richness into my life.

Some people have been called by God to be missionaries.
Now, I must object to a phrase that I have heard many
times as I have grown up within the church. When a
person announces the call of God upon their life to be a
missionary, I've often heard it said, 'Oh, God has called
them to the highest calling.' But I object to that; because
let me say this—whatever God has called you to do or to
be *is* the highest calling for your life. So all of you have
been called to God's highest calling, even if it's to be a
janitor or a service station attendant, or a grocery clerk,
or a mechanic.

You see, if I am doing what I am doing 'as unto the
Lord', my life is committed to Him. Not all are apostles,

not all are missionaries, not all are evangelists. God has called men and women to every walk of life, and it's important that we should be faithful to God wherever we are.

My wife could say, 'Kay, a mother of four children—by the will of God.' And she was faithful in mothering those children. She saw to it that never once did they get home from school without her being there. She saw to it that their lives were surrounded with love and support. She saw to it that they were taught and encouraged in their walk with the Lord and in the word of God. And as the result we've got four beautiful children serving God today, and grandchildren coming up in the same mould. We thank God that she was faithful to her calling as 'Kay, a mother according to the will of God.'

Now that the children are raised, she's become 'Kay, a teacher of younger women'—how to keep their homes and love their husbands—and God has blessed her with a very large and effective, dynamic ministry to women. Every Friday morning, over a thousand women gather as she shares with them from the richness of her own experience with the Lord, with prayer, with the word, with the raising of the family, and the raising of the children. And thank God, we see the fruit of her ministry. She was faithful in that first ministry until the children were raised, and then God called her into another ministry.

It's whatever God has called you to be that is the highest calling. And you cannot be more than what God makes you, without strain and pressure and failure.

Chuck the evangelist was a total failure. Because it wasn't by the will of God. And it wasn't until I came to the place in my ministry where I began to follow the real leading of the Spirit, and the anointing of the Spirit, and the will of God for my life, and I began to be a pastor-teacher, that I began to experience success in the ministry.

For the first seventeen years of my ministry, it was Chuck the evangelist. Though I was pastoring churches, it was still Chuck the evangelist. The churches were very small. I was not having an effective ministry at all in the lives of the people. They weren't really becoming mature in their walk with Jesus. I was giving them a diet of baby food. There was repentance from dead works, laying on of hands, baptisms—but I was not taking them into a maturity in Christ, nor taking them beyond infancy. So they remained infants, and I remained frustrated because they weren't growing up.

But it was really my fault. It was the diet I was feeding them. I wasn't being a pastor-teacher, perfecting the saints for the work of the ministry, building up the body of Christ until they came into the unity of the faith and the knowledge of the Son of God, into that fully mature person, in the measure of the stature of the image of Christ. I wasn't doing it.

But when I became Chuck the pastor-teacher, I could then say, 'by the will of God.'

Yet, you know, the amazing thing that we discovered is that when we began to teach the people the word of God, they began to grow. And as they began to grow, they began to share. Their life in Christ became evident in their workplace, in their classrooms; they began to share their faith in Christ, and soon we had evangelism like I couldn't believe!

Soon we were having people calling the church, saying, 'I wanna get saved, how do I do it?' And you can walk through the office of the church any day of the week, and hear the secretaries explaining the plan of salvation over the phone as people are calling wanting to be saved, because they've been evangelised by the church that is out in the community.

Though I am still just a pastor-teacher, and I just spend

my time teaching the people the word of God, they now, being strong in the word, are going out and sharing that word. And we're seeing hundreds of people come to Jesus every week.

I baptised over four hundred people the Friday night before we left to come to Keswick. In the earlier part of June we baptised over five hundred people. We don't have a baptistry big enough, so we go down to the ocean, and there I stand for hours as people are lined up to be baptised, and I have seventeen other pastors helping me to baptise. It's a glorious sight.

And it isn't Chuck the evangelist. I'm not preaching evangelistic sermons. But the people are *being* evangelised because the body is strong and healthy, because I am faithful to what God has called me—Chuck the pastor-teacher, by the will of God.

The addressed (verse 1)

Now, let's look at who the apostle is talking to.

1. The saints who are at Ephesus. I think it's tragic that the church has chosen certain people to canonise. Because, again, God has chosen to canonise all of you. As far as God is concerned, you're all saints. I like that— Saint Charles! I like the ring—it sounds good to me! We have all been called to be saints.

2. The faithful in Christ Jesus. So he's writing to the saints in Ephesus, and to the faithful who are *in* Christ Jesus. That phrase 'in Christ Jesus' is really the key and the theme of the book. As you go through the book of Ephesians, it's important that you underline everything that God has done for you and that you realise that it is all in Christ, or through Christ, or by Him, or through Him; and all of these blessings and benefits that God has for you are all 'in Christ Jesus'.

'And this is the record, that God hath given to us eternal life, and this life is in the Son' (1 Jn 5:11). All of

God's blessings and benefits that He wants to bestow upon you come to you in and through Jesus Christ. So what we need is the appropriating of Christ in our lives.

I love what the Lord said to Joshua as he was ready to come into the promised land: 'Joshua, the whole land is yours, and every place you put your foot, I have given it to you.' But Joshua had to go in and put his foot down—'This is mine! This is mine!' And every place he put his foot, God gave to him.

We leave much of the promised land unclaimed. We fail to go in by faith and put our foot down and claim that work of Jesus Christ and those benefits that are ours through and in Jesus Christ.

I so often hear people say, 'Oh, I've been praying that God would give me peace. I just am so disturbed and I'm upset and I can't sleep, and I'm just praying, "God, give me Your peace." ' Well, He *is* our peace. You don't need a separate gift of peace; you need more of the appropriating of Christ Jesus in your life. 'Oh, I feel like I need more love! I have such a critical attitude so often, and I don't want to feel this way, and I desire…'—No, you need more of Jesus, more of the appropriating of the work of Christ for you.

And so, as we get into Ephesians, we're going to find Paul saying in verse 3, 'Blessed be the God and Father of our Lord Jesus Christ, who hath blessed us with all spiritual blessings in heavenly places in Christ.'

All of these blessings, that God bestows upon us. And as we get into chapter 1 a little further, we'll see 'in Him', 'by Him', 'through Him', and we'll realise that all of these glorious blessings that God wants for you here at Keswick this week—all of these things that God wants to bestow upon you as you appropriate Christ, as He becomes the real Lord of your life—that these blessings begin to flow forth unto you as you become the recipient of God's glorious work.

2. His Spiritual Blessings (Ephesians 1:2, 3–7)

The expressed desire that they should experience grace and peace (verse 2)

This particular salutation is almost Paul's trademark. In every church epistle, he opens his salutatory remarks with, 'Grace be to you, and peace, from God our Father and our Lord Jesus Christ.'

In his personal epistles to Timothy and Titus, he inserts the word 'mercy'—'grace, mercy and peace'. Grace and peace have been called the Siamese twins of the New Testament, because it seems that you always find them coupled together.

I think that it is a very significant sequence: 'grace and peace', as though grace were born first, and then comes peace. You never read 'peace and grace', because that would be out of order. I am convinced that you cannot know the real peace of God within your life until you really understand and have experienced the grace of God.

I also believe that it is possible to have peace *with* God without having the peace *of* God, for surely that was my own experience for many, many years. I always had peace *with* God—that was through the work of Jesus upon the cross. But I did not always have the peace *of* God within my heart, because I did not understand the grace of God. And it was not until I came to understand it that I finally experienced the peace of God, and that's after I had been ministering for almost twelve years.

It was through my sermons on the book of Romans that I discovered the grace of God. I listened to what the Holy Spirit was saying through His word, and suddenly I realised God's glorious grace as I was preaching through the book of Romans.

My early years of ministry were, as I mentioned yesterday, spent in an evangelistic background. My sermons were all evangelistic, and I had two years' worth of them. And so I would go to a church, I would preach my two years of good evangelistic sermons, and then I would request the bishop for a transfer. And then I would do it all over again.

But I read a book entitled *The Apostle John*, by Griffith Thomas, in which he gave outline studies of the First Epistle of John. They were marvellous, expository outlines, and up to then I'd only known topical preaching. So I began to preach on that epistle. We'd never really particularly encouraged the people to read the Bible, but they found it began to come alive as they read it, and we began a series of studies which we expanded to a full year.

They weren't evangelistic sermons. However, the interesting thing was that in that year we had more people converted and baptised than any year in my ministry, in all my years of attempting to be an evangelist. There was solid growth.

But I was now coming to another dilemma: John 1 was coming to a close, and we needed a new Bible book to study. A professor at seminary had said that the book of Romans would revolutionise any church. Being a sort of revolutionary, I thought 'It would be fun to revolutionise this church. I think I will take the book of Romans next.'

I went out and bought all of the commentaries I could find on the book of Romans. I began to study it and to teach it. We spent over two years in the study of the book of Romans. I don't know about the church, but during those years I was revolutionised, because I discovered the grace of God. And with the discovery of the grace of God, I began to experience for the first time in my Christian walk the peace of God.

Grace and peace. You cannot know the real peace of God within your heart and life as long as you're trying to relate to God on the basis of your righteousness or your works.

That had been my mistake. You see, I grew up in a church of the holiness type. We were taught that we were never to drink, smoke, go to dances, go to shows—we were given all the do's and the don't's of the Christian life. Every year I would sign a little card promising before God not to do those things. I made my pledge, my commitment to God for the year.

Now, there's nothing wrong with refraining from those things. I don't think that as a child of God we should do them. However, we must not rest upon this as our righteous standing before God or the means of gaining God's favour, because it is not.

God loves me, and it is because of His love for me that He has bestowed upon me His marvellous grace.

You've heard the classic formulation, 'God's unmerited favour'. I doubt if you could improve upon it. But do we understand what it means?

There are three basic words, justice, mercy and grace, that are associated with each other.

Justice is getting what you deserve, like the sentence meted out to a criminal, or retribution to somebody who has wronged somebody else. However, when I talk to God about myself, I say, 'Mercy, Lord, mercy!' Because mercy is not getting what you deserve.

But grace is getting what you don't deserve. I don't deserve these blessings of God, this marvellous place of fellowship with Him. And yet God deigns that I should walk in fellowship with Him, so that He might manifest His love and His goodness unto me over and over again.

For years, you see, I was seeking to relate to God in such a way as to obligate God's blessings upon my life. I was seeking to make God a debtor to me, and I was looking at my righteousness as the basis for the blessings of God upon my life.

In the early years of my ministry, like Paul I often fasted. I went into the desert with my Bible and a jug of water and prepared my sermon. And then as I entered the pulpit I thought, 'Lord, surely You are going to bless this service tonight because I've been out there fasting and praying all week. And so, surely, Lord, You're going to let this be one of those kind of meetings that just flows, everybody is touched by Your Spirit and by Your love; the anointing will be so heavy upon my ministry that it will just flow.'

But it didn't work that way! I would be so weak from fasting that I would have to hang on to the pulpit to stand up, and my mind couldn't concentrate, and the service would be just as flat as a pancake. And I'd think, 'Oh, I'd better go out to the desert and fast some more...'

I was approaching God on the basis of what I had been doing, my work for him. When I discovered the grace of God, I realised that it wasn't my work for God that really mattered but God's work for me. And God in the beginning was trying to show me what grace was all about.

However, I was a slow learner, and I kept trying to do things for God. I was always trying to do something that would ensure that God would surely bless me because of what I had done for Him.

I noticed something else that I could not quite understand. Wednesday afternoon was reserved for my final preparation for the Wednesday night service. We had not been out of seminary long, and we were living on the way out from Los Angeles to Texas. There were many Texans in my seminary class, and often we had visitors. We would receive a phone call telling us friends were in town, and we would invite them over for a meal.

Often a call like that would come as I was settling down to my Wednesday preparation. I'd think, 'Oh my! I haven't got my message ready yet... hopefully they won't stay too long...' But they would sit there all afternoon, and then they would stay to dinner, and in my mind I would be thinking, 'What am I going to do? I haven't had a chance to prepare properly at all. Oh, Lord, what am I going to do?'

And they'd say, 'We'll go to church with you tonight.' Well, they're your seminary buddies; you want to really impress them, to let them think that you did learn something in seminary.

But there I was; no opportunity to prepare thoroughly. And as I walked out I'd say, 'Lord, I'm so sorry. I probably should have prepared earlier, and I'm so sorry, I'm just going to have to depend upon You, Lord. I don't have it tonight; I'm just going to depend on You.'

You know, those were some of the most powerful sermons I ever preached. The anointing and power and thoughts—everything just came together, and I was as thrilled as anybody; I knew it was just God's Spirit working in my weakness, because I was depending fully on Him.

And I thought, 'Well, now, this doesn't make sense. I go out and fast and pray all week and it's dead and flat, and here I haven't had a chance to prepare thoroughly, and it flows. It's glorious! I depend on myself—and it goes flat; I'm depending on God—and look what happens.'

God was beginning to teach me some of the lessons of grace that I hadn't yet quite learned. But I came into the discovery of grace, that God accepts me and loves me as I am, and I can relate to God on the basis of the righteousness that He has imputed to me through my faith in Jesus Christ.

I believed that. But I still thought, 'Surely I must improve on this righteousness.' I did not see myself complete in Christ. And so my endeavour was always that of trying to improve on my righteous standing, and failing to see that the fullness of the Godhead bodily dwells in our Lord, and we are complete in Him.

I was like the Galatians who had begun in the Spirit; but I was trying to be made perfect in the flesh, trying to please him with the activities of my flesh. And as a result my relationship with God was never a steady relationship but always a variable one.

Sometimes I would respond very well to a test. I would be going through a trial, and I would smile, and I would be responding so well! And then I'd think, 'Lord, did You see that? Did You see the way I responded to that one? Now, surely, Lord, You're going to bless me, aren't You, because I was so good, wasn't I?'

But there would be other tests where I would fail miserably, so miserably that I didn't even want to talk to Him. And I'd say, 'Well, Lord, I understand, Lord, I'm not asking You for anything because I know I don't deserve it...Lord, I'm not asking for a thing...That's okay, I know I'm a failure. I'm not expecting anything from You.' I was almost afraid to approach God because I'd been such a failure.

I grew up having been raised in that mentality. 'If I'm a

good boy today I get an extra piece of pie tonight at the supper; if I'm a bad boy I get sent to bed without my dessert.' And I carried it over into my attitude to God. So there was always that turmoil within, because I was always aware that I wasn't doing enough. I was always conscious of my failures, and thus I always felt slightly alienated from God.

—Until I came into the discovery of the glorious grace of God, and of that righteousness that God had imputed to me by my faith in Jesus Christ. I discovered the righteousness that I couldn't improve upon. I began to relate to God on the basis of His work and what He has done for me. And I'll tell you, our relationship has been perfect ever sense.

In my heart that striving, that struggling, with my flesh, with the failures, was over. The peace of God now reigns and rules within my heart because my relationship to Him isn't predicated on something so tenuous as my goodness or my righteousness, but it's predicated upon His glorious finished work in Jesus Christ.

And God is resting in the finished work of Jesus Christ. The Bible says 'once and for all', and God is resting in that finished work, and we need to come to rest in the finished work of Jesus Christ. 'Let us therefore fear, lest, a promise being left us of entering into his rest, any of you should seem to come short of it' (Heb 4:1).

The source of this grace and peace is God our Father and the Lord Jesus Christ (verse 2)

Now, 'The Lord Jesus Christ.'

You English people should not have as much problem with the word 'Lord' as we do in America. We don't have titles like that, and we don't understand them. But what these words are talking about is the lordship of Christ.

He brought up the subject himself. 'Not all who say,

"Lord, Lord" are going to enter into the kingdom,' He warned. So when you say 'the Lord Jesus Christ', it's important to remember that we are talking about a relationship. If He is Lord, then I am servant.

I think that Peter had a little difficulty with this. You remember when he was in the city of Joppa, and it was getting close to lunchtime, and he went up on the roof to pray. And he saw a great sheet that came down from heaven, and it had all those animals upon it, unclean animals included.

The Lord said to Peter, 'Rise, Peter! Kill and eat.' And he said, 'Not so, Lord.'

Come on, Peter, you can't say that! You can say, 'Not so, friend!', or 'Not so, Mister!' But you can't say, 'Not so, Lord!' If He is the Lord of your life, then whatever He says, you do, because He is Lord.

Jesus spoke of many who would come saying 'Lord, Lord, were we not doing all of these wonderful things in Your name?' His reply: 'Depart. I never knew you.' He never really knew them as the Lord of their lives, and that is yet what they're claiming.

Jesus is His name.

You remember when Mary was visited by Gabriel and told that she was going to be God's instrument for bringing His Son into the world? 'You shall call his name Jesus.' Later on, when Joseph was tormented and wrestling with the implications, you remember that the angel of the Lord came to him at night and said, 'Fear not, Joseph, to take Mary as your wife, for that which is conceived in her is of the Holy Spirit. And she shall bear a Son, and thou shalt call his name *Yeshua*, for he shall save his people from their sins' (cf. Mt 1:20–21).

God revealed Himself to His people by that marvellous

name of Yahweh or Jehovah, translated 'I am': literally, 'the becoming one'.

As God revealed Himself to us, as that One who becomes to us whatever our need might be, so that no matter what your need is today, you can relate to God and He'll become to you whatever you might need. Are you distressed? Are you upset? Is your heart in turmoil? He becomes Jehovah-Shalom, or Yahweh-Shalom.

Isaac said, 'Dad, here's the fire, here's the wood, where's the sacrifice?' Abraham said, 'The Lord will provide himself a sacrifice. In the mount of the Lord it shall be seen.' And after the ram was caught and they sacrificed it, he called the name of the place *Yahweh-Jireh*, 'the Lord will provide'.

He becomes the Provider.

Yeshua comes from the Hebrew name *Yeshua*, which is *Joshua*. It was a name that was given by Moses to his young minister. It was originally *Yehosua* and was then contracted to *Yeshua*, and *Jesus* is just the Greek form of the Hebrew *Yeshua*. *Shua* in Hebrew is *salvation*. Thus *Yeshua* is *Yahweh* is *Salvation*.

What an appropriate name! 'And his name shall be called Jesus, for he shall save his people from their sins.' It indicates His mission of Saviour.

The Greek *Christos*, from which we have *Christ*, is the Hebrew *Masiah*. He is the Messiah. Simon Peter said 'Thou art the Messiah—the *Christos*—the Christ—the Son of the Living God' (cf. Mt 16:16), and it was the acknowledgement that He is the fulfilment of God's promise of a Messiah, the Anointed One, who would take away the sins of the people.

Now Paul gets to the heart of his message, the thing he wants to talk to the Ephesians about.

The thanksgiving (1:3–14)

The spiritual blessings given to us in heavenly places in Christ; the beginning of the list of spiritual blessings (verse 3).

Notice, the blessings in verse 3 are 'in Christ'. All that God does and has for us is in the person of Jesus His Son.

'Thanks be unto God, he has blessed us with all spiritual blessings.' In America we have a very dangerous and unfortunate doctrine of material prosperity. To drive a Mercedes or a Rolls-Royce is a sign of your great faith and deep spirituality. It means, they say, that you've learned how to use faith, because God wants all of His children to drive Rolls-Royces; and if you're not, your faith is deficient—according to that pernicious teaching.

But I find it interesting that Paul doesn't say, 'Blessed be the God and Father of our Lord Jesus Christ, who has blessed us with Rolls-Royces and country estates and beach cottages and...' No: 'He has blessed us with all spiritual blessings in heavenly places in Christ.'

I believe that when a person is interested in God for material blessings, he is relating to God on a wrong basis. That is what Satan, when he presented himself before God, accused Job of doing. 'You've blessed him with so much. Anybody would serve You, blessed like that. Let me take away those things, and he'll curse You to Your face. Job is a mercenary,' said Satan to God.

Paul warns Timothy that we need to be careful of those who say that godliness is a way of gain. As a child of God I am interested not in the material benefits or blessings of following God, I am vitally interested in the spiritual blessings that God has for me in Christ in heavenly places, and I revel in these spiritual blessings.

Now Paul begins to make a list of spiritual blessings—it is a long one, which will occupy the first three chapters.

The book of Ephesians is easily divided into three sections.

The first three chapters are the spiritual blessings; the *wealth* of the believer. Then the second section, chapters 4 to 6:9, speaks of the *walk* of the believer. And he ends with the *warfare* of the believer. Watchman Nee divides the book in *Sit, Walk, Stand* like this: your position of being seated with Christ in heavenly places, walking worthy of that position, and then standing against the attacks of the enemy.

It is interesting that this is the sequence: he tells us of what we have, before he tells us what we should do. The weakness of my early ministry was that I was always telling the people what they should be doing. I never told them what they had—the resources which God had provided for them to be able to do what they ought to be doing. That kind of preaching is backwards, it is frustrating. You're preaching the people into conviction, but you're not giving them any answer because you're not telling them the glorious resources that we have.

Chosen in Him (verse 4)

If you were going to list all the spiritual blessings, all the wonderful things that God has done for you—which would you put first? What would be top of your list?

It is interesting to me that Paul tops his list with the fact that he was chosen 'in Christ'. Remember, it all comes in, by, through Jesus Christ. Paul was 'chosen in Christ before the foundation of the world.'

Many people find difficulty with this concept. Spurgeon, somewhat tongue-in-cheek, said, 'It is a good thing that the Lord chose me before I was born, because He would have never chosen me after I was born.'

Often when we're seeking to understand the doctrine of divine election or God's choosing, we find difficulty grasping this divine truth. The difficulty lies in our limited understanding. For God, being omniscient, knows everything. And that means He can't learn anything; for if He could learn something then He didn't know it, and therefore He was not omniscient. That means, if there is anything that is ever to be learned, it has always been known by God.

God knows all things, so that if God will ever know who was going to be saved, then He has always known who was going to be saved. There will be no surprises for God in heaven. When you come in, He won't say, 'You made it? I can't believe it!' No, God's not going to be shocked. He's going to receive you as His child, for He chose you from the foundations of the world.

Now, when God created man in His image, because He has the capability of choice He created us with the same capacity. I am a self-determinate being. I can choose what I want to do. God's choices do not violate my choices.

It was necessary that God should make me so, if I am to bring Him praise to the glory of His grace by trusting in Him. God wants a meaningful relationship of love with you. For that relationship to be meaningful, it is first of all necessary that you should be a free moral agent, or a self-determinate being—that you should have the capacity of choice. He doesn't want a mechanical expression of love, like that from a talking doll. He wants it to be meaningful. And so He gave to you the capacity of choice.

But for choice to be valid, there has to be something to choose. It was essential that God put the tree in the midst of the garden and placed the prohibition upon it. There had to be a choice, or the capability of choice would be invalidated.

And not only must there be something to choose, but the choice must be respected. The awesome thing that I have discovered is that God honours our choices. And that can be devastating when we make the wrong choice and we insist on the wrong way; God honours our choices. But it is so important to God that my relationship with Him be a meaningful relationship that, having given to me the capacity of choice, He doesn't violate that choice.

I thank God that He has given to me the capacity of choice. And I think it is marvellous that in our culture we have the opportunity of choosing the person that we are going to spend the rest of our natural lives with. I would not have liked it if my parents had said, 'That's the girl over there you're going to marry, Son.' I'm glad I had the freedom of seeing my wife for the first time and thinking, 'My! What a beautiful gal! She looks sharp!' And then of getting acquainted with her, and then of being able to ask her 'Would you marry me?' and hear her answer.

That's glorious! I love the fact that I had that choice. I would have hated to just have anybody pushed on me. After all, you're going to spend the rest of your life with that person, and it's good that you have a little bit of choice.

I'm intrigued that many who appreciate the fact that God has given them the capability of choice quite resent the fact that God also has that capacity and uses it. But— if I am interested in choosing whom I'm going to spend the rest of my life with, surely God is interested in who He's going to spend eternity with?

The problem is, I can't think as God thinks because I don't know the result of the choices. A lot of choices I've made have been wrong. When the outcome came, I thought, 'Oh, why did I choose that?' God never does that, because God has foreknowledge, and He knows already in advance what will happen.

So, how do you think when you know everything? Do you have to think? I don't know. But you see that's where God is higher than I am, and God's ways are higher than I am, because God, dwelling in that realm of foreknowledge, knows exactly...

Think of what you could do if you had foreknowledge. You could break the bank at the race track! You'd know every race—which horse is going to win. Now, if you had the capability, would you go down there and choose a loser? You'd be foolish if you did.

That's what thrills me about God. He knows the results, and He doesn't choose any losers—and He chose me. I was 'chosen in Him before the foundation of the world'—so that I might have this meaningful, loving relationship with Him.

We'll get into this further tomorrow, as we continue our study.

3. His Good Pleasure
(Ephesians 1:5-14)

If you were living in a Greek culture at the time Paul
wrote this letter, as you walked down the street greeting
your friends you would greet them with the Greek word
Charis, which is translated 'grace'. If you happened to be
a Jew, your typical greeting would be *Shalom*, as it is to
the present day in Israel, where it can be heard all over the
land as people greet each other on the street. '*Shalom*'—
'peace'.

Grace and peace.

The Lord gave me a few more thoughts on grace that I
want to share before we move on.

I never look at myself as the cause for God's blessings
upon my life. I look to Him, His love for me. Therefore, I
have learned never to make vows to God. I've found that
that is merely relying on my flesh, and failing to see myself
complete in Jesus Christ.

I have learned to expect God to bless me, though more
and more I realise how undeserving and how unworthy I
am of those blessings; and thus I have found that the
truest form of praise is that which rises spontaneously
from my heart in recognition of God's blessings of grace
upon my life.

God is so good, He has so blessed me with His blessings of grace, that as He pours out His grace and manifests His love, my heart responds to Him in praise and adoration and worship.

Sometimes I'm driving down the road, and as God begins to reveal His love and grace to me, I have to pull off the road for a while and park. It's dangerous to drive under those conditions!—just overflowing with love and thanksgiving to God, as my heart responds to His goodness to me.

I question those groups that say, 'Now, let's all praise the Lord together, because we desire God to bless us today, and we know God inhabits the praises of His people, so that we might be blessed. Let's just praise the Lord!' It's a rather selfish motive for praise. I believe that the truest praise is that which rises spontaneously from my heart as I see God's goodness and grace being bestowed upon my life and my heart just responds to God.

I have found that God does not accept—and He refuses to acknowledge—my works of the flesh. Very early in the history of mankind, when Cain and Abel brought their sacrifices to God, God rejected the sacrifice of Cain—the work of his hands—and accepted Abel's sacrifice in faith.

Later on, God said to Abraham, 'Take your only son, Isaac.'

'Wait a minute, God, aren't You making a mistake? What about Ishmael, the older son?'

God's reply is interesting. 'Your only son, Isaac.' You see, Ishmael was not the son of promise. Ishmael was the product of works, you might say. After so many years Sarah had finally said, 'Come on, Abraham, let's give up, it's not going to happen. You take my handmaid, Hagar; you go in unto her and let her conceive, and I will take the child when it's born and we will consider it as mine. It's obvious God can't work now. It's too late for Him to work.'

Have you ever come to that place in life where you just felt it was too late for God? 'God, You had Your chance. I gave You until two o'clock last Friday and You·didn't come through. Now, I'm going to have to do something about it.'

And so was Abraham with Hagar. It was the work of the flesh, and later on God refused to even acknowledge it. He said, 'Take now your son, your only son, Isaac.'

Let me add a few words about being chosen in Christ before the foundations of the world.

In the first three chapters of Ephesians, we are looking at God's side of the coin. It is interesting that the Bible always shows us both sides. It shows us God's side and then it shows us man's side. But it always shows us God's side first. And if we put the emphasis upon man's side first, we've got it out of order. It is God the initiator, man the responder. Don't reverse that! You've got it out of order if you do. So we find God's initiation in the first three chapters.

We've been chosen in Him. We're looking at the coin from God's side. Peter opened up his epistle with these words:

'Blessed be the God and Father of our Lord Jesus Christ, which according to his abundant mercy hath begotten us again unto a lively hope by the resurrection of Jesus Christ from the dead, to an inheritance incorruptible, and undefiled, and that fadeth not away, reserved in heaven for you, who are kept by the power of God' (1 Pet 3–5).

Where do you come in? That's all God's part. You have nothing to do with this up to this point. 'Begotten us again'—born again by the Spirit of God—'. . . kept by the power of God.'

No place for you yet. You say, 'Well, where is my place?'

'Through faith'. That's my place. Just believing that God is who He said He is, and that He has done what He has said He has done.

My problem is, I want a bigger place! If it's just 'through faith', I have no place to boast. I love to boast. But boasting is eliminated because God is the one who has done the work, and my part is just to believe in that work that God has done.

So, we're looking at the coin from God's side. Don't be confused and think that this is all there is. Yes, there is the other side of the coin. I must choose to follow the lordship of Jesus Christ. By faith I receive the work of God and I choose to follow Jesus Christ.

God's invitation, however, is to every man and woman. God said, 'Whosoever will, let him come, that whosoever believeth in him...' And I would like to assure you of this one thing. God has never rejected anyone who has come to Him for salvation, grace and mercy. Jesus said, 'He that cometh unto me I will in no wise cast out.'

I don't know—and I don't care—what you teach on election and predestination. It never excludes anyone from coming. No-one has ever come to God and said, 'Oh Lord, be merciful to me a sinner,' to find God replying, 'Wait a minute. What's your name? Let Me go down the list. Who? Sorry, your name's not here.'

No, it doesn't happen that way. Even though I've been chosen in Him from the foundations of the earth, the door is open to every man to come, and whosoever will come may drink of the water of life freely.

But you say, 'How do I know whether God has chosen me?' Well, there's a very simple way to discover whether or not God has chosen you. Just receive Jesus Christ into your heart and life, and you will discover that He *has* chosen you.

If you say, 'Well, maybe I don't want to do that. Maybe I don't want to accept Jesus Christ,' then there is that possibility always that He hasn't chosen you. But I can assure you, if you'll just accept Jesus Christ you'll find He has chosen you.

So, you see, we can't fault God and say, 'God isn't fair because He didn't choose me.' He has chosen all who come to receive eternal life. He has chosen that we should be holy and without blame before Him in love.

Now, let us not be guilty of making the same mistake as the Galatians, by trusting in works of righteousness that we have done.

Philip Hacking last week gave us such a tremendous Bible Reading in the book of Philippians. There in chapter 3 Paul the apostle said, 'If any man has whereof in the flesh to boast, I more,' and he gives all of the credentials that he had after the flesh. But, having listed all of these credits on the flesh side, he said, 'But those things which were gain to me'—that is, as far as a righteousness which is from the law—'those things which were gain to me, I counted loss for the excellency of the knowledge of Jesus Christ, for whom I suffered the loss of all things. But I count them as refuse, that I may know him and be found in him, not having my own righteousness, which is of the law, but the righteousness which is of Christ through faith.'

God accounts me righteous through my faith in Jesus Christ. So I am clothed today in a righteousness that I could not produce for myself. I am holy before God in that righteousness which is of Christ, imparted to me by faith. And it's glorious to realise that I stand before God today perfect and complete and without blame. Obviously, as you look at me I'm not perfect! You don't see me as perfect. But God sees me as perfect, and I am more concerned as to how God sees me than you see me.

I look at myself and I can see my imperfections. In that sense I suppose we all have magnifying mirrors. We like to magnify our imperfections, and they always look so enormous in our eyes. But the glorious thing is that God sees me complete and perfect in Christ.

Thus Jude wrote: 'Now unto him that is able to keep you from falling, and to present you'—how?—'faultless before the presence of his glory with exceeding joy' (Jude 24). So God has chosen me, before the foundation of the world, that He might work in me by His grace through Jesus Christ, imputing to me that righteousness of Christ through faith, that He sees me as holy and without blame before God in love; this glorious love that God has imparted to me, and God has imparted through me.

Predestined to be adopted as children by Jesus Christ (verse 5)

God has adopted us as His children by Jesus Christ. He has made us all sons 'according to the good pleasure of His will, to the praise of the glory of His grace.'

Because God has done this for me, I cannot take any credit, praise or glory. It is only to God that we can give them. As we sing: 'To God be the glory, great things He hath done.'

I can't go around boasting of what I am or what I've done. I can only boast in the Lord and what He has done, and that's the way God wants it, that it might be to the praise of the glory of His grace, that through ages to come we will be praising God for His wonderful glorious grace to us, having adopted us, placing us as His sons by Jesus Christ.

In whom we have redemption (verse 7)

To understand the word 'redemption' in verse 7, you have to go back into Hebrew culture, and into the Old Testament. For there are our first references to redemption. The laws of redemption are given to us in the book of Leviticus. We find there that redemption applied to individuals and it applied to property.

If you owed a debt and were unable to pay it, then you could be sold as a slave, and you would have to work off that obligation. However, a family member could come along and pay the debt. He would be your *go'el*, your kinsman-redeemer. Or, during the time of your slavery, he could pay off that debt and redeem you from your slavery.

Property could be redeemed also. It was extremely important to the people that property should remain within the family. Each family as they came into the land received their inheritance, and it was important to them that the family maintained that inheritance. So, whenever you sold a field, when the deed was drawn up and sealed, there were always the revisionary clauses within the deed, whereby in a specified period of time, by fulfilling certain requirements, you could redeem the property back for yourself, or back for the family, so that it would remain within the family.

There is a classic example of the law of redemption in the book of Ruth. You remember the story of this Israeli couple, Elimelech ('My God is King'), and Naomi ('Pleasantness'); this couple who, because of circumstances—a prolonged drought—decided to sell their field near Bethlehem and move over to the other side of the great Afro-Syrian rift, to the Moab mountains.

And so, with their two sons, Mahlon and Chilion, they made their journey to Moab. Now, the name Mahlon means 'sickly'; the name Chilion means 'pining'.

Quite often the Israelites would name their children after the circumstances of their birth. When Rebekah had her twins, the first one came out all hairy, and so they said, 'Call him "Hairy" '! And so he was named Esau, which means 'Hairy'. When his brother came out, he reached out and grabbed Esau's heel. And they said, 'Look at that! He's a heel-catcher. *Ya'qob!*'—one who catches another by the heel in order to overcome him.

Evidently when the children of Elimelech and Naomi were born they didn't look very healthy. So they acquired their names. And *My God Is King* and *Pleasantness* moved to Moab with *Sickly* and *Pining*. While they were living in Moab, Sickly and Pining married a couple of Moabitish girls. But because they were sickly and pining, they both died before there were any children born. Also, Elimelech died.

And so Naomi, you remember, called her two daughters-in-law to her and said, 'Girls, I'm going home. I've had so much grief in this land, I just can't stand being here any more. There are too many memories. You girls can return to your parents. I'm too old to ever produce other children for you to wait for them to grow up and marry; and so I relieve you of any sense of obligation. Go home, and I pray that God will help you to find husbands, and I hope that you'll have lots of children and be blessed.'

You remember how Orpah fell on her neck, kissed her, and left; but Ruth said to her, 'I beg you not to ask me to leave you or to forsake you, or to return from following after you, because wherever you will go, I will go. Wherever you will live, I will live. And your people will be my people, and your God will be my God. And God forbid if anything but death should separate us.'

So Naomi came back with Ruth to Bethlehem, and all the people said, 'Oh, have you heard? Naomi's back again? Oh, hi, Naomi!' And she said, 'Don't call me

Naomi, "Pleasantness", call me Marah, "Bitterness" '—
for, she said, 'God has dealt bitterly with me.'

Having come back, they were in poor circumstances,
but God established a very interesting and, I believe,
marvellous welfare programme. Under the law, when you
harvested your fields, you were only allowed to go
through the fields once to pick the fruit. Any fruit that
wasn't ripe had to be left on the trees, and later on the
poor of the land could come in the orchids and pick that
fruit. When you went through to harvest your grapes, you
could only go through once. Any of the fruit that wasn't
ripe had to be left on the vine, and later the poor of the
land could come in and take that fruit. When you were
harvesting your fields, you were allowed just one cut with
the scythe, and if it didn't cut clean or was bent over, you
had to leave it; you couldn't take the second stroke. And
as you were gathering the wheat, if you happened to drop
some on the ground, you couldn't pick it up. It was left for
the poor of the land.

So the poor of the land would follow the gleaners
through the fields to pick up what was dropped, bent over
and not cut cleanly. And that way the poor were taken
care of.

It was decided that Ruth would go out into a field and
glean after the harvesters. And it so happened that she
came into the field of the man whose name was Boaz. And
she gleaned all morning.

At lunchtime Boaz came out. He was talking with his
workers, and he happened to notice the young lady among
the gleaners, and he said, 'My! Who is that?' And they
said, 'That is Ruth, the Moabitess who returned with
Naomi from Moab.' And he said, 'Well, ask her to come
over here.' So they went over to her and said, 'Boaz would
like to talk with you.'

He said to her: 'Now, I've heard of the marvellous

things you've done for your mother-in-law, and I want you to know that I admire and respect you for that, and I have ordered my servants to let you drink from their containers. So whenever you get thirsty, just come and drink of the water that they have drawn, and at lunch you can take your bread and dip it in their soup. And remain in my fields.'

After she had gone he said to his workers, 'Don't you lay a hand on that girl. And if she should happen to wander over in the fields where you haven't yet harvested, don't rebuke her. And every once in a while, when you see that she's behind you, let a handful fall on purpose for her.'

So when Ruth came home that evening with a bushel of grain, Naomi said, 'Where in the world were you gleaning today?' And she said, 'Well, it so happened that I was in the field of a man whose name was Boaz.'

And Naomi said, 'Honey, you stay in that man's fields. Don't you let him catch you in any other field. You remain in his fields, throughout the harvest.'

That year Ruth harvested a bumper crop. But they were coming now to the time of the threshing, and so Naomi said to her, 'Now, look, tonight you go down and stand back, watch them there as they're eating, and note carefully where he lies down to sleep. And when he has settled down, slip in and take his blanket and cover yourself with it. If he asks you about it, just say, "I want you to cover me with your blanket." '

There was an interesting provision in Jewish law. It actually preceded the law, but was incorporated into it. It concerns the preservation of the family name. If a man should take a woman as his wife, and if he should die before there were any children, his brother's responsibility would be to take that same woman as his wife, and the first child would be named after the dead brother to preserve his name in Israel.

Now, that could be a bad thing, if your brother had married some really unsuitable girl. So they did have a provision by which you could get out of it. You could come to the judges at the gate of the city, and you could say to the judges, 'This woman was married to my brother who died without any children, but I don't want to have anything to do with it.'

Then you would take off your sandal and you would hand it to her. She in turn would spit in your face. You would receive a derisory title: from then on you would be called 'the man from whom the shoe was loosed in Israel'. It meant that you were a man who didn't stand for the family honour and didn't care to carry on the family line.

Now, Elimelech was dead; his two sons were dead. The family name was about to die. But Boaz was a brother of Elimelech, and that's why Naomi was so excited when she said it was the field of Boaz. And that's why Naomi said, 'Go down and take his blanket and cover yourself with it.' Because, in reality, it would be the obligation of Boaz, under the law, to raise up a son through Ruth to carry on the family name.

So Ruth went down and hid in the shadows. After everybody settled down for the night, she slipped in, took his blanket—his skirt—and covered herself.

About midnight or so, he woke up, his feet were cold, and he realised that there was someone lying at his feet.

'Who's there? Who is it?'

And she said, 'I'm Ruth, the Moabitess.'

'What are you doing here?'

'I want you to cover me with your blanket.'

'Oh my! Oh, I would love to, but there's a problem,' he said. 'There is another brother who is closer kin than I am, and he has the first rights of refusal. But you get back to

Naomi before it gets light. Don't let anybody know that a woman was here on the threshing floor tonight, and in the morning I'll see what I can do.'

Bright and early in the morning, Boaz was sitting in the gate of the city waiting. When his brother came passing by, he said, 'You remember our brother Elimelech, who with Naomi sold their field and moved to Moab? The rights of redemption are coming up on that field now, and you have the first right to redeem it.'

His brother said, 'Well, that's great! I think I'll do it!'

Boaz said, 'There's just one hitch. Whoever redeems the field will have to raise up a son for Elimelech through Ruth.' He said, 'My wife would never understand that! Why don't you redeem the field?' And he took off his shoe and handed it to Boaz, passing on the right to him. Boaz didn't spit in his face though, because he wanted Ruth.

So Boaz redeemed the field and took Ruth as his bride, and she bore a son, and they called his name Obed, who bore a son whose name was Jesse, who bore a son whose name was David the great king of Israel.

But now, why did Boaz redeem the field? Because he wanted more property? No. He redeemed the field because he wanted the bride. He was in love with Ruth. He wanted the bride, and so he redeemed the field to get the bride.

As we move over into the New Testament and Matthew's Gospel, we encounter the kingdom parables. 'The kingdom of heaven is like unto treasure hid in a field; the which when a man hath found, he hideth, and for joy thereof goeth and selleth all that he hath, and buyeth the field' (Mt 13:44).

Now, of whom is it speaking? Well, first of all, what is the field? Expositional constancy tells us that the field is the world. Who, then, gave everything to purchase the world? Jesus Christ. In fact, His purpose was to redeem the world.

You remember when Satan took Him up into a high mountain, showed Him all the kingdoms of the world, and said, 'Look! I will give all of these to you, and the glory of them, if you will just bow down and worship me. For they are mine, and I can give them to whoever I will.'

Jesus had come to redeem the world. He said, 'The Son of man has come to redeem, to seek and to save that which was lost.' His mission was redemption. But it was to be through His blood. Why did Jesus redeem the world? Because God wanted another world? No. Look out on the universe and see the vast expanse of galaxies, and realise that each of them could have their own solar systems, and the billions and billions of planets. God didn't need another planet. There was a treasure He was interested in. There was a Bride, and He was in love, and in order to get the Bride, Jesus redeemed the world, to get the treasure.

And so we read in Revelation chapter 5 concerning the scroll, the title deed to the earth, that John saw a scroll written on the inside and out and heard an angel proclaim with a strong voice, 'Who is worthy to take this scroll and loose the seals?'

John said, 'I began to sob convulsively because no-one was found worthy in heaven and earth to take the scroll or to loose the seals, until the elders said, "Weep not, John; behold, the Lion of the tribe of Judah hath prevailed to take the scroll and loose the seals," and John said, 'I turned, and I saw him as a Lamb that had been slaughtered, and he came and took the scroll out of the right hand of him that sat upon the throne. And when he did the elders came forth with their little golden bowls full of odours, which are the prayers of the saints, and they offered them before the throne of God.

'And then they sang a new song saying, "Thou art

worthy to take the scroll and loose the seals, for thou wast slain and hast redeemed us by thy blood, out of every nation and kindred and tribe and tongue and people, and thou hast made us unto our God kings and priests, and we shall reign with thee upon the earth" ' (cf. Rev 5:1–10).

Glorious redemption! God has purposed that you should be a part of His eternal family, and to that end we have been redeemed by the blood of Jesus Christ from our life of slavery to sin. Jesus has set us free, He has paid the price of our redemption. He redeemed the world, that He might take you, His treasure out of it—you, with whom He was so much in love.

So when I come to this verse 7—'In whom we have redemption through his blood'—I think of the glorious love of Jesus Christ for you and for me, that caused Him to pay the price, that He might redeem us from this corrupt evil world, that He might make us His children, that He might lavish upon us His love, world without end.

Oh how glorious! He chose me! And having chosen me, He redeemed me by His blood, that I might share eternity with Him in the glories of His kingdom. Thank God for redemption through the blood of Jesus Christ!

4. His Workmanship
(Ephesians 2: 1–10)

As we were preparing to come to Keswick this year, the Lord gave to us the twenty-third Psalm. 'He causes me to lie down in green pastures, beside the still waters. He restoreth my soul.'

I'd like just to say what a blessing it's been for us to be here, in the green pastures, by the still waters. I know how the Lord has restored our soul—it has been a joy and a blessing to have shared this time with you.

This morning I would like to give you a brief outline of chapter one, going over the territory we would have liked to have covered.

Paul opens his letter to the Ephesians with the salutation (in verses 1 and 2). Then he gives thanks to God for spiritual blessings in Christ in heavenly places (verse 3).

Beginning with verse 4, he tells us some of these spiritual blessings. He will go on with the list through chapter 3, making reference to them. But in verse 4 he tells us that we were chosen in Christ before the foundations of the world.

Verse 5: We were adopted as His children.

Verse 6: We were accepted in Christ—in the Beloved.

Verse 7: We have redemption through His blood.

Verse 7: We have the forgiveness of our sins.

Verse 9: He has given to us the knowledge of His will.

Verse 11: He has given to us an inheritance (Peter speaks of 'an inheritance incorruptible, and undefiled, and that fadeth not away, reserved in heaven' (1 Pet 1:4) for those who are being kept by the power of God).

Verse 13: We have been sealed with that Holy Spirit of promise.

The first prayer of Paul for them (1:15–21)

The prompting of the prayer (verse 15)

Then Paul prays for the Ephesians, and in his prayer he describes two qualities, or characteristics, of the church (verse 15): He speaks about their faith in the Lord Jesus, and, secondly, about their love to all the saints. These two go together. A true faith in the Lord Jesus will manifest itself in a love for all the saints.

We have a habit of wanting to pick and choose those whom we will love, perhaps those who are of our own denomination; and yet the Ephesians had the love for all the saints.

Interestingly enough, the real proof that the church gives to the world that we are His disciples, is that we love one another. And though a person may boast of all kinds of spiritual gifts and spiritual abilities, and service and sacrifice for God, if they don't have this love, it's meaningless; it doesn't say a thing. The tongues are no more than just a clanging sound.

It is also interesting that, as John points out to us in his first epistle, not only is our love for each other the sign to the world that we are His disciples, but it is also the sign to us that we have passed from death to life—because we love the brethren.

Tragically, some thirty years after Paul wrote his letter to the Ephesians, Jesus also wrote to the Ephesians by the hand of John. 'And unto the church in Ephesus write these things' (Rev 2:1). Though the church was still functioning, still going on with its works, yet there was one vital characteristic that was missing from that church some thirty years later. Jesus said, 'Nevertheless, I have this against you. Though you've maintained doctrinal purity, though you've maintained your works, yet you have left your first love.'

The characteristic that Paul mentions—their love to all the saints—was something that was missing in the next generation. And we hear those words of Jesus of warning, declaring, 'Unless you repent and return to your first works, I will remove your candlestick out of its place,' or, 'I will take My presence from that church.'

It's tragic. The church was once noted for its love for all saints. Within a generation, we see that gentle rebuke from Jesus, because they had left that first love.

The petitions of the prayer (verses 17–19)
Paul offers his prayer that God would give them 'the spirit of wisdom and revelation in the knowledge of him' (verse 17).

It is important to realise that I cannot really know God, except by the revelation of the Holy Spirit and the revelation of the word as the Spirit opens it to my heart.

One of Job's friends in their discourses said to him, 'Who by searching can understand God unto perfection?' The natural mind cannot know the things of God, for they are spiritually discerned.

And so Paul prays for that work of the Holy Spirit, in giving them the spirit of wisdom and revelation in the understanding and the revelation and knowledge of Him.

That they might know God, first of all. Secondly, *that they might know the hope of His calling* (verse 18). If you only knew the glorious hope of that calling—God has called us as His sons and daughters—if you only knew what this hope was, this inheritance that we have in Christ!

That they might know, thirdly, *the riches of the glory of His inheritance in the saints*. It's not the riches of our inheritance; he wants us to know how much God treasures you. Peter says that you are His 'peculiar treasure'. I do find it rather peculiar that God should place such value on me; that He should consider me His treasure. And of course we remember that in Malachi they who loved the Lord spoke often one to another about Him, and God eavesdropped, and He kept a record, and they shall be accounted as His jewels in that day. God just loves to have you talk about Him. Any time you do so, He listens in— He wants to hear what you have to say about Him. And God accounts that as treasure; 'His inheritance in the saints'.

Oh, if you only knew how much God valued you! If you only knew how much God treasured you! And that's what Paul is praying—'God, help them to know just how much You love them, how much You treasure them.'

And then he wanted us to know *the exceeding greatness of God's power* (verse 19) that is made available to us who believe. All of the power that you need to live a successful life in Christ is imparted to us by the Spirit, and hence his prayer that you might know this power that is available to you who believe.

It is a power that raised Jesus from the dead. It is a power so great that it was able to set Him on the right hand of the throne of God on high. It is a power that is above all other powers in heaven or on earth.

Then Paul points out, in chapter 1:5 and 9, that all of these things were done by God according to His good pleasure, and (verse 11), according to His purposes.

In other words, God is the initiator. God is the one who

has initiated His love, His grace, His goodness, towards us. And it was all done that it might resound to the praise of the glory of His grace (verses 6, 12 and 14) and made available to all of those who trust in Him.

The grace of God (2:1–13)

But now, Paul wants to show us the grace of God.

As an artist, desiring to paint a picture for us of the beauty and the glory, the brilliance, of the grace of God unto us, Paul felt it necessary to first of all splash the canvas with a dark background, so that the colours can be fully appreciated when he places them on the canvas.

To whom the grace revealed (2:1–3, 12)
Firstly, *Those who were dead in trespasses and sins* (verse 1).

He paints, first of all, this black, dark background, because he wants to splash on it brilliant colours of grace. That black, dark background is you, before God began His work in your life, and you who were dead in trespasses and sins.

Way back in the beginning, God said to Adam, 'Of all of the trees that are in the garden you may freely eat, except the tree that is in the middle of the garden—and in the day that you eat thereof, you shall surely die.' The consequences of sin, the consequences of transgression, is death. Under the law, God declared, 'For the soul that sinneth, it shall surely die.' And Paul tells us in Romans, 'For the wages of sin is death.' This of course is spiritual death, which is a separation of a person's consciousness from God.

The Bible has another definition for death, one that is used mainly in our medical sciences today: the separation of a person's consciousness from his body. We call that 'clinically dead'. You look at the little chart upon which the E.E.G. is monitoring, and when the brain-wave activity goes flat, they take away the artificial equipment because they say they are clinically dead; there's a separation of the consciousness from the body. That's one biblical definition—it says, 'And he gave up his spirit.' It's a reference to death.

But there is another biblical definition of death, and that is the separation of your consciousness from God. And that is always the effect and the result of sin. As Isaiah said, 'God's hand is not short that he cannot save, neither is his ear heavy that he cannot hear, but your sins have separated you from God.'

Now, there is a difference between sins and transgressions. The word 'sin' in its root meaning means to miss the mark. We must acknowledge that not all missing the mark is deliberate. You can just be a poor shot. I know many people who are suffering because of their inability to be what they feel God would have them to be. The Bible says that all of us have sinned and come short of the glory of God. John tells us that if we say we have no sin, we deceive ourselves, the truth isn't in us. We've all missed the mark. But we thank God that the blood of Jesus Christ is cleansing us from all sin. And even though John wrote 'that we sin not', he said, 'And if we sin, we have this advocate with the Father, even Jesus Christ the righteous, who is the propitiation for our sins.'

I know a lot of Christians who are struggling with the weakness of their flesh. There is a missing of the mark in their life, and they hate it, they cry to God, they pray, they would love to be freed from that plaguing failure in their life. It's good to know that God knows our frame, and He knows we're but dust, and He has made provision for the weaknesses through the empowering of the Holy Spirit, as we struggle to come to that place of the reckoning of the old man to be dead.

But the fact that it is a reckoning indicates that it's a position of faith. Unfortunately, I still am going around in this old body, and thus I groan and travail with all of creation, as I'm waiting for the manifestation of the sons of God—the redemption of this body. It's terrible to be carrying this old, stinky carcass around, but such is the case until God sees fit to redeem the body. And as long as I am in this body, the motions of sin will be with me. Thank God, I don't have to yield to them, but I often do. But thank God, when I do, I have Jesus Christ the propitiator of my sins. He is my advocate, and His blood is constantly cleansing me from all sin.

Transgression is a little different. That is wilful, deliberate disobedience. God has said, 'Here's a line. Now, I don't want you to go over that line.' What will you do? It's a deliberate choice. If you choose to cross the line, that's a transgression.

But both sins and transgressions bring death. You were dead in your trespasses and sins. You had no real vital consciousness of God.

Secondly, *Those who in times past walked according to the course of this world which was being directed by Satan*. And in times past, he said, we walked according to the course of this world. This Greek word, translated 'walked', in its root meaning, is 'meander'. There's another Greek word for 'walk' which means 'to walk with a steady gait'.

When you see a person meandering, you are first of all inclined to think that they're just wasting time, that they're not getting anywhere. They're without purpose. Do you realise that before you came to a knowledge of Jesus Christ, you were meandering through life because you really didn't have any purpose? You weren't going anywhere. It's not until Jesus Christ comes into our life that He gives us a real meaning for life and a real purpose to live.

The word 'course' in the Greek of verse 2 goes back to the roots of the Greek word from which we get the word 'weather-vane'—the indicator that points wherever the flow of air is going.

Now, the world has a flow. They call it fashion, and it's amazing how many people are victims of fads and fashions. Wherever the flow, the current, of the world, that's where they go, and they flow with it.

I remember my mother telling me, 'Honey, you're going to have to realise that as a Christian, as you go through life, for the most part you're going to be going against the current. And it will be a lonely walk.' She said, 'Just remember, any dead fish can float down the stream; it takes a live fish to go upstream against the current. And you'll need that life of Christ to go against the current.'

I thank God for a mother who gave such sage advice to a young boy who wanted to flow with the course of this world.

But that is the way that life was before Christ! Just flowing, meandering, wherever the direction and flow of the world is going.

But the frightening thing is that the flow of the world is being directed by the prince of the power of the air, who is even now working in the children of disobedience. Satan is behind the world's fashions, behind the worldly music. It used to be that he tried to subtly hide himself. No more! Those acid rock groups, they're up front with their satanic worship symbols and everything else. Satan has really come out of the closet and he is demonstrating the fact that he is behind the flow of the worldly fashions. He is called the god of this world, controlling fads—the fashions of the world.

And at one time, we were following that flow, that

spirit which even now is continuing to work in the world around us, among whom all we once did live that way, in the times past.

Thirdly, the grace was revealed to *those who were children of obedience as they lived to fulfil the lusts of the flesh and the desires of their minds* (verse 3), and, fourthly,

To *those who were by nature the children of wrath* (verse 3). For our lives were marked by the fact that they were controlled not by the Spirit of God but by the lusts of our own flesh. That was the controlling factor—living after the flesh, fulfilling the desires of the flesh and of the mind, and thus we were the children of wrath even as others.

Fifthly and sixthly, the grace was revealed to *those who were without Christ, aliens and strangers* (verse 12), and to *those who were without hope and without God in this world* (verse 12).

There is the black background.

From whom the grace was revealed (2:4)

Now Paul's going to splash some bright colours of love and grace and mercy and the kindness of God on this black background.

Verse 4: 'But God...' Oh, thank God! This is that transition that brought us from darkness to light, from death to life, from that place of despair to hope. 'But God, who is rich in mercy, for his great love wherewith he loved us...' The mercy of God, the love of God—and when? 'Even when we were dead in our sins...'

Oh, how important that we realise that. God didn't start loving me the day I raised my hand, or the day I went forward. We remember that when the rich young ruler came to Jesus: 'Jesus looked upon him and loved him.' Yet he went away sorrowful because he couldn't pay the price. That didn't stop the Lord from loving him. God loved us—even when we were dead in our trespasses and sins, even when we were rebelling.

'Herein is love, not that we loved God, but that God loved us, and God manifested his love toward us; even while we were yet sinners, Christ died for the ungodly.'

How Satan loves to take and beat Christians to death with a couple of verses in Hebrews. Like, 'God just is through with you! God doesn't care for you! You have failed God too much!' And 'God is just so upset and disappointed with you.' And we fail to realise that God loved me when I was in rebellion.

And if, when we were at enmity with God, we were saved by the death of Jesus Christ, how much more now shall we live by that life of Christ, by the resurrection and the life of Christ within us, shall we live unto God by that power and by that life. If God loved you when you were in rebellion, and was willing to give His mercy and love and kindness and grace in Christ to you, how much more now that you're a child of God, is He understanding of our weaknesses and of our failures! He is so tender, He is so gracious, He is so compassionate, and, again, He knows our frame, that we're but dust.

We're so many times disappointed in ourselves. God isn't! God knew that weakness was there all the time, and many times had to bring the circumstances to reveal that weakness to me.

I thought I was strong! I thought I didn't need any help! I was in a dangerous position, so God put me through a test, let me fail completely, and I said, 'Oh God, I'm so sorry. I thought I had it made. I thought...'

'You have to trust Me, Son.'

In every area where I had self-confidence, God had to test me, to show me my weakness, to show me that my trust must be absolutely in Him, so that where I was weak, now I am strong, because I'm not trusting in myself, I'm trusting in Him—His mercy and His great love.

When did God love us? Even when we were dead in trespasses and sins! And thus He made us alive together with Christ. For by grace you're saved.

How the grace was revealed (2:5–6)
Now come the bright, bright colours of grace on the canvas.

By making us alive together with Christ (verse 5); *By seating us together in heavenly places with Christ* (verse 6). 'For he has raised us up together...'—go back to chapter 1—'...He has seated Christ in the heavenly places, far above all the principalities and powers.'

And what was His purpose?

The ultimate purpose of His grace (2:7)
'...That in the ages to come he might show the exceeding riches of his grace in his kindness toward us through Christ Jesus...'

In Christ Jesus, by Christ Jesus, by Him, through Him, in Him!

Faith the agency by which grace received (2:8)

'For by grace are you saved through faith...', says Paul, and then makes an interesting statement—'...and that not of yourselves.'

You know, God knows how incurably boastful we are. He knows that man is desiring to be worshipped. And we love to boast of what we have done. So God doesn't leave anything to us whereof to boast of. He even gives us that faith to believe—'For by grace are ye saved, through faith, and that not of yourselves, it is the gift of God; not of works, lest any man should boast.'

Think if it were not that way; think, if we could earn our way to heaven; think if we could start earning points, and we could earn our way into heaven; think of what a miserable place heaven would be. All of the boasting going on when we got up there! And I'd sit there listening to you tell your stories, all of your exploits and wonders for God and all, and I'd think in myself, 'Oh what a bore! I wish you'd shut up so I could tell them how wonderful I am!'

But when we are there by the grace of God, all we can do is bow our head in wonder and in reverence, and say, 'Oh, thank God for Jesus Christ. He paid it all—all to Him I owe.'

Not our works for Him but His work in us (2:10)

I'm there by the grace of God only—'Not by works, lest any man should boast, for we are his workmanship.'

You see, that's the key. It isn't really my work for God that counts for anything, it's God's work for me that means everything. I am His workmanship.

The word 'workmanship' is an interesting Greek word that the translators have always found difficulty translating, and thus you find the various translators translating that 'handiwork', 'workmanship' and 'work of art' and other definitions like that.

The Greek word, though, is a very simple word. It is a word *poema*. In a direct transliteration of it, we get our English word 'poem'. We are God's poem. What is a poem? A poem is a work of art. And the artist is always desiring to express himself in his work, whether he be a sculptor, a painter, a composer, or whatever, you've got something within that you're seeking to express so others can see the beauty and the glory of it.

And you are God's expression, you're His work of art, as God is seeking to express Himself through you to the world. And that's the work of God that's going on in my life, as He is conforming me into the image of Christ, that

He might through me express Himself to the world around me.

'For we have been created together in Christ Jesus unto the good works that God has before ordained that we should walk in them.'

What Paul is saying is that God is working in you today to prepare you for the work that God has for you to do for Him in the future.

For years and years God was working in my life to prepare me for the work that God had in mind for me to do for Him. God allowed me to go through years of difficulty and hardship. God allowed me to spend my early years just spinning my wheels, with no success at all from the ministry.

God allowed me to go through those experiences of seeing that it wasn't me, it wasn't my personality, it wasn't something that I could do; so that when He finally prepared me for the work He wanted me to do, that He had before-ordained that I should accomplish for His glory, when He started to bring the people in by the thousands and then by the tens of thousands—there was no way that we could stand and declare some marvellous programme, or whatever. All you can say is, 'It's God's glorious doing, it's God's work.' And you're not about to stand up and try and take credit for what God is doing. Because you know what you could do: nothing!

For seventeen years God allowed me to have to work on the side in order to support my family, so I could stay in the ministry. He allowed me to do that for seventeen years. But all the while He was teaching me how to be careful with money. He taught me how to be frugal. He taught me how to live a simple life. God knew that one day He would channel millions of His dollars through my hands to touch a world for Christ. And what a thrill it is to be able to have these resources that God has now given to us. We have the privilege of spending millions of dollars every year for the work of Jesus Christ around the world.

But all the while, you see, in those years of hardship and difficulty, working, often wondering where we were going to get money for the evening meal, God was working in me, preparing me for the work that He had already ordained that I should accomplish. I wish I had known then. It would have been a lot easier on God had He told me! Because I gave Him a bad time in those years! 'Lord, why do You allow me? Lord, why can't You...?' I was just struggling, struggling, struggling—and yet, God in His wisdom had a plan all set out.

And He has a plan set out for your life, and those hardships and difficulties and all that you're going through now, are all a part of that necessary preparation as God is preparing you. You are His workmanship, and God is preparing you for that work that He has already ordained that you should accomplish for His glory.

God bless you as He works in you, and as you discover the purposes of God, the plan He has for your life.

THE ADDRESSES:
ONLY ONE THING IS NEEDED

by Rev. David Jackman

Luke 10:38–42

We've come to Keswick from all over the country, and doubtless from all over the world. We've also come from a wide variety of churches, traditions and backgrounds. And yet as we've gathered, we've been reminded already by the banner behind me that we are 'all one in Christ Jesus'.

We've had a sense of that even more clearly this year, in the events of Mission 89. I'm sure that many of us were among the million and more people who attended the meetings. Some of us may have been among those who went forward to make a public response to the preaching of the gospel through God's servant, Billy Graham. All of us will know people whose lives have been transformed and touched by the word of God through Mission 89; and in that we greatly rejoice together.

And now here we are at Keswick. Not an evangelistic event primarily (though the open-airs are a very important part of what we do during this week), but primarily a discipleship Convention.

Perhaps you wonder what the Keswick Convention really is all about. Over the years, it's been defined as a time when we come together in order to understand more clearly what practical biblical holiness really means, and how—by God's grace through the work of His Spirit in our lives—we can grow in that holiness. Or (if you want to put it in a rather more up-to-date way) how each of us can become more like the Lord Jesus in our character, behaviour, and every aspect of our lives.

Now, is it self-indulgent to come away for a week to think about that? I want to suggest to you that it isn't so at all, but rather that it is essential; because following Mission 89, the churches to which each of us belong have to nurture the converts and instruct the enquirers, as the Holy Spirit continues His gracious work of making disciples of the Lord Jesus.

Dr Billy Graham has gone, but that great task continues, and it is an awesome responsibility. Not just because of its size and complexity, but also because we all tend, by the sort of discipleship that we model, to produce others in our own likeness. And *that* is a responsibility that ought to make every one of us humble and dependent upon God.

You know the old rhyme:

> What sort of a church would my church be
> If each church member was just like me?

What it's really asking is: what quality of discipleship will be modelled by the people who came to Keswick in 1989—here this week, and as we go back at the end of the week?

I once saw a poster on a student's bedroom wall that asked: 'If you were arrested for being a Christian, would there be enough evidence to convict you?'

That's what this week at Keswick is about: practical, biblical Christlikeness.

So we turn to Luke's Gospel chapter 10. It's a chapter all about discipleship. At the beginning, Jesus appoints and sends out thirty-five (or thirty-six, according to which text you follow) pairs of disciples to go ahead of Him announcing the kingdom of God. It was an important message (verse 16). They were going as Christ's messengers to proclaim the coming of the King, and Luke tells us that the seventy-two returned with joy, thrilled with all that they had experienced of the power of the Lord in conquering the enemy.

But notice what Jesus says to them in verse 20. 'Don't rejoice that the spirits submit to you, but rejoice that your names are written in heaven.' In other words He directs these disciples—who've been thrilled in this early evangelistic mission in which they've had a part—away from activity *for* Him back to their relationship *with* Him. 'Rejoice that your names are written in heaven'—because that's what discipleship is all about.

In verse 22, Jesus explains that being a Christian disciple means learning who the Father is through the ministry of the Son. It's coming to know God personally through Jesus Christ.

The second half of the chapter explores this idea of discipleship further. In answer to the question asked by the expert in the law (verse 25), Jesus replies 'What does the law say?'

'Love the Lord your God,' the expert answers, 'with all your heart and all your soul and all your strength and all your mind, and love your neighbour as yourself.'

Jesus goes on to tell that story of the good Samaritan, illustrating the second of those commandments: 'Love your neighbour as yourself.' And right at the end of the chapter (verse 38), Luke inserts this little story about Mary and Martha, illustrating the first.

Loving God with all your heart and soul and strength

and mind: that's our focus this evening. Because that's where we've got to begin, if we're ever going to have an impact on our world.

I wonder what you've left behind to come to Keswick? I am not really thinking about the tomatoes that you hope your neighbour is going to water for you! I am thinking about the hundred-and-one loose ends and unfinished tasks that (if you're anything like me) you've left behind: the letters that we should have answered; the people we might have visited; the books which we wish we'd read; the help that we wanted to offer.

Many of us have come to Keswick carrying around with us an invisible briefcase, full of unresolved problems, loose ends, frustrations, and unfinished business so pressing that I guarantee many of us have brought that briefcase into this meeting tonight. And more than once you've had it on your knee and opened it, and started to go through it all, since this meeting began. That's what we've come from.

Several years ago Charles Hummel wrote an important article entitled *Tyranny of the Urgent*. He suggested that we all need a thirty-hour day to cope with life, but remarked: 'But would a thirty-hour day really solve the problem? Wouldn't we soon be just as frustrated as we are now with our twenty-four-hour allotment? Our dilemma goes deeper than shortage of time. It is basically the problem of priorities.'

Doesn't that ring a bell with you? The problem of priorities.

Let me suggest three important lessons from these few verses tonight. Firstly, Jesus shows us some

Significant symptoms

Martha was distracted by all the preparations that had to be made. She came to Him and asked, 'Lord, don't You care that my sister has left me to do the work by myself? Tell her to help me' (verse 40).

Now, Martha's often had a bad press, hasn't she? Sometimes she's been represented as thoroughly worldly, almost unworthy of having Jesus in her home.

I don't think she was like that at all.

Her name, literally, means 'mistress', and that seems to have been her natural role in the home at Bethany. She seems to have been the organiser. It was she who took the initiative, as verse 38 tells us, in welcoming the travelling teacher into her home. It was she who wanted to meet the need of Jesus with her loving gift of hospitality, and it was a generous warm-hearted action of love towards the Lord Jesus.

She was a fine friend of Jesus, and we know from John 11 (the story of the death of Lazarus) that she was also a devoted servant of the Lord Jesus. Martha is not someone to be written off at all!

But when we meet her in verse 40, she is quite frustrated because she has a problem of priorities. And she is out of sorts, in a number of directions and a number of ways.

1. She's out of sorts with Mary

If you'd gone up to her that day and asked, 'Now, Martha, just wait a minute, what is the matter?', she would have said: 'Well, firstly, the matter is Mary. Look at her sitting there doing nothing, when there's so much work to be done! I wanted to do my very best for the Lord. It's such a privilege to have Him in our home. But there's been the guest-room to prepare and the food to be bought, and it's got to be prepared and it's got to be served. And then there's the washing-up to be done, and as soon as you've finished washing up for Him and all His disciples, there's the next meal to prepare. And you would have thought that Mary might have helped, wouldn't you? But no—all she does is enjoy herself sitting at His feet, talking to Him. It's just as well somebody in this house is practical and gets on with things!'

Martha is resentful and jealous, even bitter about her sister. That is always a significant symptom that something is wrong: when frustration makes us critical and bitter and jealous of our brothers and sisters.

'I've been left to do the work by myself,' she says. How many of us are tired and frustrated because we think we're constantly being put upon, that more and more is demanded of us? We're never really appreciated for what we do. We're so busy in Christian service that we're worked off our feet. And, if anybody could look into our hearts, they would find that we're just full of self-pity.

2. She's out of sorts with Jesus

But if you'd gone on to ask, 'Is that the whole problem?', she would have said 'No: it's Jesus that's wrong.'

'Lord, don't You care that my sister has left me to do the work by myself? Tell her to help me!' She wasn't only out of sorts with her sister—she was out of sorts with her Lord as well.

The one often leads to the other. And I am sure that I'm talking to somebody here who honestly, before God, is out of sorts with the Lord. You've got a grievance against Him. You've brought all sorts of unresolved problems to Keswick with you, and you don't know why God doesn't seem to see or care; and if He is such a God of love and mercy, why doesn't He do something about the situation that we are up against?

But all that Jesus seems to do, as we read this passage, is to encourage Mary by going on talking to her. So Martha determines to correct the situation. She will come and tell Jesus what to do (verse 40, end).

It doesn't seem to have occurred to her that the Lord had His priorities, and that they didn't match hers. When our own spiritual priorities are wrong it doesn't occur to us, does it? When we find ourselves telling God what He ought to do about our circumstances, church, family or future—'Lord, why don't You do this?'—then it's a very significant symptom that the relationship is skewed, that we're not in a right relationship with God.

'Don't You care?' she said.

Of course He cared. Whenever you turn on God and ask that question it's a sign that you've got it wrong. Those disciples in the boat who, earlier in the Gospel, said to Jesus in the storm 'Don't You care that we're going to drown?'—they got it wrong. They hadn't reckoned on His authority, His power, His ability to say, 'Be quiet' and 'Down!' to the waves.

And yet I guarantee that many of us are saying that in our hearts at this moment: 'Lord, don't You care?'

So if you'd gone to Martha and asked, 'What's the problem, Martha?', she would have said, 'It's her and it's Him.' But the Bible says, it's Martha. Because,

3. She's out of sorts with herself
This is a very significant symptom. In verses 40 and 41 there are three words describing Martha.

She was distracted. The verb literally means she was 'drawn away'. She started off listening to Jesus. She welcomed Him into her home. She began to hear what He was saying. But then as she was sitting listening, she allowed her thoughts to wander. Maybe she'd had a hard day. And she began to think about the cooking that was waiting to be done.

It's a privilege of a minister sometimes to visit homes. Sometimes you're sitting chatting to your host and hostess, and suddenly you realise the hostess has pulled out of the conversation. And a minute or two later she's slipped out of the room; and you know that she was thinking about the meal. Now she's just going to have a look at it, just make sure it's ready, to just do that little bit extra.

She was drawn away.

Oh, she really wanted to listen to Jesus, but there was so much to be done! And serving Jesus became a greater priority than being with Him. Is that a symptom you recognise?

So there she was, out in the kitchen on her own, distracted.

She was worried. Another interesting verb; it means 'drawn in different directions'. She really wanted to be in there with Mary, but she couldn't be; and so she was torn, because she'd got her priorities wrong.

And we're worried in the same way whenever we say: 'Well, I really would like to have that regular time alone with God. I really do mean to read my Bible every day and pray—but, you know, my life's terribly busy and demanding, I just can't seem to fit it in. And all my spare time seems to be taken up with church committees, or leading my house group, or going out with the evangelistic team and knocking on the doors, and nobody else seems to bother. Somebody's got to do it.'

And inside us, there is a turmoil that inevitably expresses itself outwardly, because we are being torn apart by priorities that others are writing for us, while Jesus has different priorities for us.

She was upset. That's a strong word too. It means 'to be thrown into an uproar', and it has the root meaning of 'stirring up trouble'. The distraction and worry within her bubble up to the surface, so that she says, 'Lord, don't You care? Tell her to help me.' The head of steam finally explodes, and all her frustration and anger pour out, because the real problem isn't Mary or Jesus, it is Martha.

Before the Second World War there was an extensive

correspondence in *The Times* about what had gone wrong with the world. Lots of people wrote in suggesting solutions to the problems the world was facing. The correspondence was closed by the editor after the shortest letter had been published. It was written by G.K. Chesterton, and he simply wrote, 'Sir, what's wrong with the world? I am. Yours faithfully, G.K. Chesterton.'

That's where we've got to start.

I would be very surprised if there were not many of us here at Keswick spiritually distracted, worried and upset. Perhaps you're a missionary and you've come home frustrated and exhausted by the work that you've done, and, really, as you look at everything, it seems as though the Lord doesn't care and He hasn't been fair with you; and, is it really worth it all? Or you may be a minister or a Christian worker in a church, and you're facing so many difficulties and misunderstandings; and you begin to wonder, 'Does He really care? I'm so busy.'

Wherever you are and whoever you are, when you are empty and tired and defeated and frustrated, let me ask you: is the problem really Mary? Is the problem really Jesus? Or is the problem really you, Martha?

The divine diagnosis

What is Jesus' response? Verses 41 and 42: 'Martha, Martha,' He says.

Notice how personal and gentle the Lord's loving rebuke is. 'Martha, Martha, you are worried and upset about many things, but only one thing is needed. Mary has chosen what is better, and it will not be taken away from her.'

You see, what Jesus is doing in His love for Martha is to make her question her own assumed priorities. Twice we are told that she is over-stretched.

Verse 40 tells us she is distracted by 'all the preparations'. If you translate that literally, it would say, 'She is
distracted by much deaconing'—that is, household work.
A deacon was a waiter at the table, a server of others.
And Martha was distracted by all the work she was doing.

Jesus goes on to say in verse 41, 'You're worried and
upset about many things, but they are not necessary
things.'

She had a false idea of what Jesus needed. Her whole
emphasis was on how she could serve the Lord Jesus, but
Jesus gently showed her that her own need was much
greater. It's not Martha meeting His need that's important, it's Jesus meeting her need. And the only real neces-
sity, the only thing He really wants from Martha, is that
she should allow Him to minister to her.

We need to let that sink in. That's the diagnosis that
God gives. You see, our greatest danger is that we will
allow what we consider to be urgent to crowd out what the
Lord Jesus considers to be important.

He says to her, in effect, 'Martha, I don't need all this
food. You're doing too much that I haven't asked you to
do and that I don't need.' Much service is not in itself
pleasing to God, if He has not asked us to do it. It is very
possible to do more than Christ has asked us to do, so that
we omit the very thing that is needful.

You see the difference in priorities. Martha looks at
Jesus and sees somebody who needs a meal. She wants to
serve Him—but that takes over everything. Mary looked
at Jesus and saw someone who could meet her own deepest need for God, and everything else faded into insignificance.

And yet, you see, Martha's motivation seemed so right,
didn't it? Jesus doesn't rebuke her for being busy—He
wants us to be active, serving, disciples—but He rebukes

her for doing what He hasn't asked and for not doing what He *has* asked for.

I want to say to you, at the beginning of this Convention, that the only way to be a disciple of Jesus is to do what He asks you to do. And that is, to sit at His feet and listen to what He says. Martha, bless her, couldn't fit that in. She didn't have time, because it wasn't important enough to her.

I wonder, has God brought us to Keswick to get that sorted out? One thing is needful. And what is that one thing? Well, it's the good part that Mary has chosen; it is to sit at His feet, listening to His word.

When we get to chapter 18 of Luke's Gospel, we find a young man who is also told that one thing is needful. 'Go and sell what you have, give it to the poor, and follow me.'

Both Martha and that young man were told that the one thing that Jesus wanted from them was that they should do what He'd told them to do; that His priorities should become their priorities.

Alan Redpath used to speak, sometimes from this platform, about 'the barrenness of a busy life'. It is an acute danger for Christians that, as life speeds up more and more, we all tend to get over-stretched.

Many of our churches suffer from lack of strategic thinking and planning to fulfil Christ's priorities. Many of our Christian leaders suffer from the pride that thinks that we're indispensable, from an unwillingness to train others as a priority in our ministry, from the pressure of other people's expectation. Many of us live lives that are totally undernourished and virtually exhausted spiritually, because so few Christians today make the priority of Jesus their priority; to sit at His feet and listen to what He says. And fewer still obey what they hear.

That's the divine diagnosis; that's what He wants from us.

His radical remedy

We need to end our study at verse 39, with Mary, who sat at the Lord's feet listening to what He said.

Let me ask you, does that sound too simple, too inactive?

Think again. Mary had grasped the great privilege that was hers. You see, no Jewish woman would normally be able to sit at a rabbi's feet. No rabbi would have allowed her to do it. No rabbi would allow a woman to become a disciple. The rabbis taught that a woman's place was in the kitchen. Martha was doing the right thing as far as they were concerned.

But that was not where Jesus wanted Martha or Mary to be. All that could come later. His priority is not to eat, but to teach. Our priority is not to be busy, but to learn. The one involves being God-centred, sitting at His feet listening, active in obedience. The other involves being self-centred, making up our own mind what we want to do for Him, and becoming frustrated and distracted and anxious and worried.

How many of us who teach others serve up scraps, because we don't discipline ourselves to the hard work of hearing Him speak in studying the Scriptures? Mary made a choice, Jesus said—'She has chosen what is better.'

And so must we. And that requires discipline. It's much easier at the end of the day, rather than spending time in prayer, to switch the television on for an hour and then drift off to bed. It's much easier in the morning, by the time we've washed and dressed and had our breakfast, to say, 'Well, there's not much time for the Bible today.' It's much easier just to read a page of inspirational thoughts from some Bible notes, rather than to really grapple with God's word, to take time to sit at His feet and say, 'Lord, what do You want to say to me?'

That's why our discipleship is so weak and why we're so

distracted and anxious and upset. Mary's choice shows that she was totally dependent on Jesus. That's the whole point. As she sat at His feet and listened to His word, she was really saying, 'I am utterly dependent upon the Son of God. I must have His instruction and His direction for my life.' And I want to say to you that that is the only way to the fulfilment of your own human and Christian potential. We'll always be out in the kitchen, alone and frustrated, if we don't make time to sit at His feet and listen to His word.

There is much debate today about how God speaks to us. Many of us use the words 'The Lord told me' very easily, and sometimes far too lightly. But amid all the debate about *how* God may speak to us, let's recognise at Keswick this week that we can be sure that God always does speak when we open His word, the written Scriptures, and ask their author the Holy Spirit to make that word live in our lives.

God may choose to speak to us in other ways, but He is always committed to speaking through His word. The Scriptures testify with one voice to the living Word, the Lord Jesus Himself, and the Spirit of God still takes the word of God to speak to the people of God.

And so we're not here at Keswick to look inside ourselves for some sort of inspiration or hunch about what God wants us to do. We're here to sit at His feet, to look up into the face of Jesus with our Bibles open, and say: 'Lord, You gave this word. Speak to me. I want to know Your truth. I want to know Your direction for my life. I want to know Your priorities so that I may do them.'

We dare not neglect the sure and certain word that God has given us. For what Scripture says, God says, and what God has said He is still saying.

So says the Bible, 'Today, if you hear his voice, do not harden your heart.' Why does it matter so much that we should be here listening to the word of Jesus? Because when I hear His word I shall get everything else in my life into perspective. I shall understand what He wants me to concentrate on, and I shall learn His priorities for my life, and begin in the strength of His Spirit to live that life.

Isn't that why we've come to Keswick? We want to listen to Jesus. And the promise is that if that's what we really want, He won't take it away from us. 'Mary has chosen the better part and it will not be taken away from her.'

Even death itself cannot sever the communion and fellowship with the Lord which we find in this world, as we get to know Him through His word and listen to His voice as His Spirit teaches us. One day all our serving will be over, but our relationship with Him will never be over. That is the better part, that will never be taken away. If you invest time in listening to God in His word you are investing for eternity.

So I want to be very practical as I close, and I want to invite you in this opening meeting, with me, to make Mary's choice our choice with three simple personal resolves.

1. I will seize the opportunity
I want us to say together to the Lord Jesus tonight, 'Lord, I am going to seize the opportunity.'

Jesus and the disciples were in transit (verse 38). It was an all too brief visit, but Mary was determined to make the best use of it. And Keswick is a unique opportunity— for some of us, once in a lifetime. Thousands upon thousands of people have seized their opportunity in this lovely little town, because Jesus is here. Don't let it pass you by.

2. I will refuse to be distracted
Secondly, my resolve is to refuse to be distracted; to leave that invisible briefcase containing my frustrations and

loose ends at the 'Left Luggage' counter. Don't let it stop you from hearing His word!

You may say, that's escapism. It isn't, it is spiritual realism. You will come back to your briefcase far better able to cope if you leave it in 'Left Luggage' while you listen to Jesus.

Be ready to invest the time to do so. And remember that it's not just as a member of this great crowd, but as an individual that He speaks into your life. Often it is in the crowd, in a meeting like this, that you'll hear Him speaking with great clarity and authority to your situation. But it may equally be on your own, in a quiet place by the lake, up in the hills, in your tent or in your room, as you say, 'I'm not going to be distracted, I'm going to get alone with Jesus. I'm going to open my Bible and listen to His word.'

3. I will be ready to obey

'Disciples' means 'learners', and we've all got much to learn about ourselves, about our false priorities and about what God wants to do in our lives.

But, my friends, we also need to do it. And we shall find it's only as we depend on Him that His word will begin to work out in our lives. That's why the place to start and the place to end is at His feet, listening to what He says: 'Speak Lord, Your servant hears.'

Will you make those resolves with me as we close our meeting this evening?

THE DANGER OF DRIFT

by Canon Keith Weston

Hebrews 2:1

I had the great joy of being in Australia with my wife in
January for the Keswick Convention near Melbourne.
Afterwards we were able to visit Tasmania. There was a
reason in my heart for wanting to go there, because my
great-great-uncle emigrated to Australia and ended up in
Tasmania, having been soundly converted in England;
William Pritchard Weston inherited money, squandered
most of it in riotous living, and then, in some way or
other, when he was seventeen or eighteen, he got soundly
converted.

In Launceston Museum in Tasmania there are six boxes
of his memoirs, and I had great fun reading through the
first chapter of an unpublished manuscript recounting his
conversion and his twice-shipwrecked voyage to Australia. In his testimony he says that he learned to exchange
the pleasures of the playhouse for attendance at the house
of God. He went on from strength to strength, built two
churches in Tasmania, was a much respected citizen of
that land and eventually became Prime Minister.

He was converted the same night as another man mentioned only by his initials A.B. Their careers later diver-
ged; William went off to Australia, and A.B. stayed in

Britain. William was later horrified to hear that his friend had drifted from his profession of faith. From initially doubting the great truths of Scripture, he went on to deny the deity of Christ and become a Unitarian.

A.B. became an accountant, and began to embezzle his firm's funds. Out of kindness to him, his employers tried to hide the fact that they knew what he was doing, to keep him out of prison. But eventually they had no option but to report him to the authorities, and he was imprisoned, placed in shackles and—would you believe it!—sent to Australia in chains as a convict.

And those two careers illustrate what I want to say to you tonight for the Lord.

You may be somebody—I trust you are—who looks back to the day when you were soundly converted to the faith of the Lord Jesus Christ; maybe very recently through the ministry of God's servant Dr Billy Graham, or maybe years and years ago. But where has the path of your pilgrimage led you from there? Where have you gone since? For the question we're asking tonight is: 'Is there drift at any point in our lives?'

'Lest we drift away,' says the writer to the Hebrews. Because drift is the great danger that besets so many Christians in these days.

We've heard that moving address about how the loving Lord Jesus restored His servant Peter from failure.[1] Peter, to whom was entrusted a marvellous ministry; but have you asked the question, 'Why was he a failure? Why did Jesus have to restore him?'

In the Gospel account, Jesus warns him: 'Simon, Simon, behold, Satan hath desired to have you, that he might sift you as wheat. But I have prayed for thee' (Lk 22:31). And I believe the Lord wants to say to many of us here tonight, 'Listen: Satan desires to have you, to sift you like wheat, to draw you away from My discipleship, to destroy you. And I am praying for you.' The love of the Lord Jesus desires to reach out to some in this tent, who may be in great danger of drift. For 'Satan desires to have you.'

Are we so naive as to think that when we commit our lives to the Lord Jesus Christ, Satan remains disinterested? I tell you, he is bitterly opposed to everyone here who is a disciple of the Lord Jesus Christ. He will use every and any device to bring down you as a believer, and his ultimate aim is your destruction.

That's a sobering thought, isn't it? But Scripture says that if we're involved in spiritual warfare, then we've got to gird up our loins; lest you, dear brother, dear sister, begin to drift from the truth as it is in Jesus, and find yourselves in the hands and chains of Satan.

Now, let me immediately put that in the glorious context, not only of the loving prayers of the Lord Jesus for every one of us, but also that of the finished work of the Lord Jesus Christ by which our redemption is secured; and through whom 'we are more than conquerors through Him that loved us' (Rom 8:37), saved by the blood of Christ and 'kept by the power of God through faith unto salvation ready to be revealed in the last time' (1 Pet 1:5).

Such is the security that we're meant to enjoy as Christians, so that with the apostle we can joyfully say at the end of Romans 8, 'If God be for us, who can be against us?...Who shall separate us from the love of Christ?' (Rom 8:31,35).

Yet I fear that there may be such a failure to grasp these glorious truths and to understand and articulate the faith upon which we stand, and such an ignorance of some of its majestic truth—and, moreover, such an attitude of carelessness and fickleness and prayerlessness on the part

of so many of us who are Christians today—that we may
fail to keep our guard up. And we shall drift.

'For our adversary the devil walks about seeking who is
the next one to devour,' as Peter's statement (1 Pet 5:8)
should be translated. And only a fool fails to be properly
aware of the fact.

Paul says, 'We are not ignorant of his devices' (2 Cor
2:11). I feel I want to reply, 'Paul, are you sure?' Because
so many people these days seem to be ignorant of Satan's
devices, and they trip lightly through life thinking that
Satan is not interested in them and all will be well. But the
writer to the Hebrews writes 'Lest we drift', and that's the
whole line he's pushing in his epistle again and again:
'Beware, beware, beware, lest you drift.'

Satan's devices are very subtle, and the danger of drift I
think is the greatest subtlety that he could trail in front of
us. He's too subtle to often indulge in head-on confrontation. Oh, he will do it from time to time, but so often the
head-on confrontation comes after months, maybe years,
of temptation to drift.

His main strategy is one of quiet, almost imperceptible,
undermining of a Christian's resolve in Christ. To loosen
his grip on the truth, to snip away at the convictions he
thinks he holds. To seek to lower the Christian's defences,
until the point comes—oh! so imperceptibly, so progres-
sively subtly—that we may be only vaguely aware of what
is happening.

May I address that to some of you who are new Christians here tonight? God bless you—but will you watch out
for Satan's tactic of sowing doubt in your mind? The
subtle suggestion that what's happened to you is all a
concocted dream? That the truth can be questioned to the
point where it looks quite ridiculous?

You see, that's what happened in Genesis 3. It's all
there in Scripture; the progressive, almost friendly way, in

which Satan undermined Eve's knowledge and understanding of God: 'Did God say?' And Eve replies, quite correctly, 'Yes, He did say,' and she quotes Scripture.

But the doubt has been sown, and it gnaws away until Satan can say to her, only a few verses later, 'You will not die.'

'Oh, but God said, 'You will die''—but Satan denies the truth, and Eve believes his lie.

Will you beware, then, of the subtle indoctrination of Satan? I believe many, many Christians, if they're honest, are finding their faith crumbling beneath them. Drifting is a very real possibility. I believe that the same tactic is often used by Satan against the mature Christians. Such a person's faith and grasp on truth may seem to him, as he comes to a Convention like this, like an impregnable pillar of granite—the granite truth of the gospel. He knows it; and he has taught in Sunday School, and preached for years, and he knows that truth and nothing he believes can shift it.

But Satan, I think, chips quietly away so often at the very foundation of such a solid upbringing in the truth. A suggestion made here or there—containing a veiled temptation, you hardly notice the thought that's being seed-planted in your mind, but it's a temptation that becomes relished and enjoyed.

Outwardly the big Bible is still there and the reputation of being a very respectable Christian, but in the mind the corrosive atmosphere has become something which is hard to get rid of. And when the mind is idle, it turns back to the day-dreams based on the temptation that Satan has put in there.

James says it all in his epistle, doesn't he? A train of thought that would once have been appalling even to entertain becomes almost a habit in the mind. And then, says James, that Christian has become 'double-minded' and 'unstable in all his ways' (Jas 1:8). The great granite block of conviction has been subtly chipped away, and then comes the head-on invitation to commit the sin. And such has been the subtle undermining, the sowing of these seeds of dissent in the mind, that suddenly that respectable, upright, well-thought-of Christian crumbles in an appalling sin. Very often Satan loves to do this in the realm of sexual ethics.

Is Satan chipping away at the impregnable rock of your stand on the truth of the gospel, so that you know, if only you're honest with the Lord, that it is beginning to crumble and is in great danger? 'Lest you drift', you've got to do something about it.

Lot, you remember, chose the fertile valley where Sodom and Gomorrah were, and went and lived there (Gen 13:11). There have been addresses preached at Keswick on this sad and sorry progression, or rather regression. One verse later, he moves his tent 'toward' Sodom. In the next chapter, he is dwelling in Sodom. Six chapters later, it says he sat 'in the gate of Sodom' (19:1). In other words, he was an elder of that wicked city.

Drifting, drifting. No doubt he justified it. 'I can cope, thank you very much. I wouldn't dream of doing the things that Sodom and Gomorrah do! How could you suggest that I would? Oh, I'm no fool; don't you know?' He might even have convinced himself that he went there as a missionary to do some good. But no: it was pure self-interest and stupid ignorance.

And what once might have been unthinkable to Lot, whom Scripture persists in calling righteous, becomes that which brings him to the very brink of destruction. 'Now,' says the writer to the Hebrews, 'We ought to give the more earnest heed to the things that we have heard, lest we drift'—because the seed is there in our hearts; the possibility exists that we might drift.

Where will you be forty years from now, young man, young woman? That was a question asked by Basil Atkinson at the Christian Union of the college which I attended. 'Where will you be forty years from now?'

The writer to this group of Hebrew Christians is most concerned for these readers. His concern mirrors the Lord's love for people like us, because He knows all about us. The things that we so successfully hide from others are all naked and open before the Lord, and yet He loves us. 'He knows the worst about you,' says the old chorus, 'and He loves you just the same.' He pleads with you—lest you drift.

The writer sees his readers as Christians with such an immature grasp of the truth that they're desperately in danger of losing that grasp. So, what does he do? He feeds them with marvellous expositions of nourishing, refreshing and strengthening truth.

That's the whole context; look at chapter 1. The things that he says we must pay more heed to are the glorious truths about our majestic Saviour, exalting Him (in chapter 1 of this epistle) in a way which leaves you almost breathless with wonder.

'Now,' he says, 'hold on to that, lest you drift.'

God has spoken all down the ages, he says, 'in many varied ways' (Heb 1:1). That message was valid—that's the word in the RSV (2:2)—and accompanied by sobering warnings for those who would not give heed and obey the message. 'But,' says the writer, 'in these last days he has spoken to us by his Son'—and He a person of such majestic character and presence, because He's God in person, in this world, bringing God's message Himself, that all the previous prophets and the very angels pale into insignificance as bearers of the message. It's God who's spoken to you.

'For unto which of the angels said he at any time, 'Thou art my Son'?' (1:5). Therefore we must pay the closer attention to the things that He, God, has said to us, lest— can it be possible?—we should drift away from it.

And the very fact that the warning is there, means that there is an appalling possibility that you, dear brother, dear sister, may be the target of Satan's activity to make you drift from it.

Commentators have some interesting things to say about Hebrews 2:1. Let me share three of them very briefly with you.

Firstly, the Greek word used for 'drift' here is used nowhere else in the New Testament. It's a word which the writer has particularly chosen. In classical Greek it has various meanings. For example, it can mean *letting something slip away through your fingers*—like water escaping from your hands as you're trying to drink, or dripping from a leaky vessel. Dripping away, perhaps almost imperceptibly; letting something slip from our grasp.

The Revised Version (probably one of the most accurate versions of the New Testament) opts for this meaning. There is even a footnote: 'i.e., run out as from leaking vessels'. One might imagine the desperate scene in the camp of a French foreign legion, heavily outnumbered in the desert and running out of ammunition. In a lull in the attack the legionnaire reaches for his waterskin to slake his thirst because he's desperate for refreshment. And, to his horror, the last of the water has leaked away because the skin has been pierced by gunshot. There's no water left.

That's the feel of the Greek. 'Hold on to what God says

to you in his covenant. Don't let it slip through your fingers, lest in the moment when most you want to stand upon the promises of God you cannot. Think for a moment what they are.'

Do you see that application? The writer to the Hebrews is saying, 'Listen, you dear friends; take heed, great truths are at stake. What your soul depends on, Satan is trying to rob you of. You must pay attention, you must value that truth, you must store it away in your hearts. Your eternal destiny depends upon it. And in the heat of battle with Satan—with 'the world, the flesh and the devil'—you are going to stand, because the promises of God are secure in your grasp. And you're not, by carelessness or stupidity, letting those promises slip from your grasp.'

Notice the emphasis. Three times, in 3:7–8, 3:15 and 4:7, he quotes from Psalm 95, like a tolling bell: 'Today, if you hear his voice, do not harden your hearts.' Is that a danger in which you stand? What if God speaks to you this very day, at this very Convention, about something that is absolutely vital to your eternal destiny?

But the meaning of this phrase in Greek is not just 'like fluid dripping away through a leaky vessel', it also means *letting go of something*—perhaps by your own carelessness, almost without noticing that it's gone. Like dropping your handkerchief. In classical Greek it's used of a ring slipping off a finger and being lost.

I was at a Convention once where that actually happened to the wife of one of the speakers. They'd gone for a walk on the beach, and when they got back they discovered to their horror that her wedding ring was missing. Now, she knew she had it because she always wore it. She also knew that it was getting loose on her finger and that something needed to be done about it. But nothing had been done and now it was gone.

It was full of precious significance, not least because they'd been married for many very happy years. It spoke eloquently of the promises that they'd made to each other at their wedding all those years ago. And now it had slipped off her finger and was gone. Surely it was impossible that she would ever find it again.

And 'impossible' is the word used in this letter: 'It is impossible to restore again to repentance those who have once been enlightened...if they then commit apostasy,' says the RSV, 'since they crucify the Son of God on their own account and hold him up to contempt' (Heb 6:4,6).

Later in the letter, you read of Esau (12:17). When he saw what a fool he'd been, he sought repentance with tears, but he couldn't repent.

And these uncomfortable verses are placed among the chapters of Scripture 'lest we drift'.

I agree with you, chapters 6 and 10 are two of the great difficult chapters of the Bible. I've wrestled with them often. How do they fit with the assurance and security that a Christian has in the love of Christ?

I leave that as your homework! But don't leave them out just because they're difficult chapters—lest you drift, and you enter into that impossibility of repentance.

That's a sobering thought, brothers and sisters. Doesn't that shake you?

I want to tell you that actually that wedding ring, astonishingly, was found. The tide had gone in and out twice, but the members of the houseparty, having prayed about it, found it on the beach the next day.

Peter, the failure, becomes Peter the man entrusted with tremendous responsibility in ministry. Oh yes, God is so gracious!

But watch it, watch it! Satan would have you drift.

The third meaning of the Greek word 'to drift' is, if

anything, even more sobering. It's used of a boat *drifting from the place where it's supposed to be moored.*

I once visited the Niagara Falls. Above the Falls, only a few hundred yards upstream, was the large black hulk of a barge which had broken free from its moorings and got stuck on the rocks right in the mainstream, heading for disaster. One couldn't help wondering how it came to be there. Had it broken loose from a mooring, or from a tug that was towing it? Was it full of valuable cargo when it broke adrift? Was there panic amongst the people who saw it drifting down towards Niagara Falls?

That's the background to this verse, 'Lest we drift.'

The great stake to which God would have us securely moored is the unshakable covenant word of God. What danger, then, if we drift from it through carelessness, slipping our mooring, so to speak, until we, having grasped the truths which belong to our salvation, are swept away by the currents, perhaps currents of theological opinion, or of secular moral standards that are contrary to the word of God. And we are tugged and pulled and tugged, until the mooring slips and we drift to disaster. That's the picture.

If you read it in context, it may be even more sobering, because as you read on in Hebrews the writer writes to us in chapter 4 about the rest into which God desires and purposes us to enter. But such is the tortuous power of Satan's influences upon us that we may be swept away from that harbour where He would seek to bring us. There is the harbour where we belong for all eternity, but to our horror we find ourselves being pulled past it and missing the rest that God intended us to enjoy.

In 3:12, he writes to Christians, 'Take care lest there be in any of you an evil, unbelieving heart leading you to fall away from the living God.' In 4:1 he warns 'While the promise of entering his rest remains, let us fear lest any of you be judged to have failed to reach it.' And in 4:9 he writes 'There remains a sabbath rest for the people of God. Let us therefore strive to enter into that rest, that no-one fall by the same sort of disobedience'—that is to say, characterised by some of those pilgrims in the days of Joshua who never entered into the rest, but perished in the wilderness.

These are sobering thoughts to share. I don't enjoy them. But as God looks at us this evening, is there anyone in this tent to whom this warning has to come tonight? Sin is being entertained in your life and you know it. And God says today, 'If you hear my voice, harden not your heart, lest you drift,' and the implication is, 'drift to destruction'.

I must close.

Would you dare to pray the words of Psalm 139 after a talk like this, this evening? To go to some quiet place and dare to say to God, in all honesty, 'Search me, oh God, and know my heart; try me and know my thoughts, and see if there be any wicked way in me, and lead me in the way everlasting'? It may be that we would be almost too scared to pray that, in case He should put His finger on the one thing that we know so well He's spoken to us about again and again and again.

But brethren and sisters, 'We must pay the closer attention to what we have heard, lest we drift away from it.'

1. This address by Rev. Jim Graham immediately preceded the present one by Canon Weston in the evening Convention meeting. The tape is available from the Keswick Tape Library (see p.255), no. 89/14.

CLEANSED, FREED AND FILLED

by Mr Peter Maiden

Hebrews 10: 11–18

In this passage of Scripture two things are mentioned, for which I believe millions in the world and thousands in the church are longing.

Before we look at them, let's note the context. The writer is referring to the Old Testament sacrifices. He argues that if they had made the worshippers perfect, then why do the priests go on offering them time and time again, year after year? If those sacrifices could have purged the worshippers, then, verse 2 tells us, the worshippers would have received two things. They would have been cleansed once for all, and, secondly, they would no longer have felt guilty for their sins.

I believe that millions in the world and thousands in the church are longing to experience what the Old Testament sacrifices could not do for people: to be cleansed, once and for all. To have the knowledge firstly that they stand clean and forgiven before a holy God; and, secondly, that they no longer have to carry with them through this life a burden of guilt.

Continuing with his argument, our writer says that not only did those sacrifices fail to give cleansing, not only did they fail to deal with guilt—they actually did the very opposite. In verse 3 he points out that they were an annual reminder of sin.

Take, for example, the instructions for testing an unfaithful wife, which Moses gives in Numbers 5:11–31. He states that if a man suspects his wife has had an illicit relationship, he is to bring her to the priest with an offering, which would be used as part of the process of discovering whether or not she was guilty. The name of that offering is interesting. 'It is a grain offering for jealousy, a reminder offering to draw attention to guilt' (verse 15).

And that, says our writer, is what these annual sacrifices did. They drew attention to guilt. The worshippers saw that the sacrifices were still necessary. They reminded them of the sins they had committed, and showing them by their very repetition that it was (in the words of verse 4) impossible for such sacrifices to take away sins.

I wonder how many present at this Convention meeting are struggling with guilt? Some fall into sin, which has made you nervous even of the presence of God; some besetting sin, or just some weakness, some inconsistency in your Christian life that causes you shame. To use last night's words[1], maybe you sense that you have been drifting away.

Satan is a great reminder, isn't he! He has an amazing ability to constantly bring those sins before our eyes, and to stifle and to stanch the joy and the freedom which is our birthright as the children of God. And I have come to this platform this evening simply to tell you that Satan is a robber. He is a thief. He is stealing that which is rightfully yours—your birthright as sons and daughters of the living God.

So let's see together how complete cleansing and complete freedom from guilt are rightfully ours.

The writer takes the matter up in verse 11. He pictures again the Old Testament priest standing and performing his duties, offering those sacrifices which, rather than taking sin away, seem to remind the worshipper of his guilt.

Our writer sees the fact that the priest stands to perform his sacred duty as very significant. His work in the sanctuary was never complete. He could never rest, and the worshippers could never rest either. They knew that the sacrifice that they were witnessing had to be followed by another, and then by another.

Note also that now our writer is not speaking of annual sacrifices, as in the first three verses. He's speaking of daily sacrifices—daily reminders of sin, daily reminders of the burden of guilt that those worshippers had to bear.

How we should thank God for the twelfth verse of this chapter! 'But when this priest had offered for all time one sacrifice for sin, he sat down at the right hand of God.'

I want to suggest to you that complete cleansing, absolute freedom from guilt, is ours—because of four very simple realities which we see in this passage.

The Priest who is ours

Our Priest is the Christ (verse 5). He is the one who now sits at the right hand of God (verse 12). He is the one who perfectly fulfilled the will of God. Listen to His own words: 'I have come to do your will, O God' (verse 7). We know from other Scriptures that our Priest is God's beloved Son with whom He is well pleased.

And it is this man who is our Priest, it is this man who made an offering for our sins—a cleansing offering, because of the Priest who is ours.

The price which He paid

And we're told in verse 12 that He made one sacrifice for sins. Verse 14 assures us that that one sacrifice has 'made perfect for ever those who are being made holy'.

One sacrifice that satisfies, for ever, a holy God. We look back to millions of sacrifices under the old covenant which failed to take away sin, but this one sacrifice we are assured deals with it—once and for all. And you may well ask, 'What kind of sacrifice must this be?'

Look at verse 5—'Sacrifice and offering you did not desire, but a body you prepared for me'; verse 19—we 'enter the Most Holy Place by the blood of Jesus'; verse 20—'through the curtain, that is, his body.'

To fulfil God's will to the uttermost meant the offering once for all of His own body and blood. The body which the Father prepared for Him at His incarnation, He now freely offers to God as a sacrifice. And the glorious news of the Christian gospel—which Satan will do all that he possibly can to hide from the human race, and which he constantly seeks to cause even God's people to doubt—is that this offering is entirely and completely acceptable to God.

That truth has brought the very best out of our hymn-writers. Listen to Augustus Toplady:

The terrors of law and of God
With me can have nothing to do;
My Saviour's obedience and blood
Hide all my transgressions from view.

Or Charles Bancroft:

Because this sinless Saviour died
My sinful soul is counted free,
For God the just is satisfied
To look on Him and pardon me.

So, what is the result of this great work which Christ has done on our behalf?

Well, quite simply, what the Old Testament sacrifices just could not do, Christ has done. Remember their weakness? They could not take away sins (verse 11). But Christ's work has done just that: it has taken away our sins so far that it's as far as the east is from the west.

It is, in Spurgeon's words, 'an incalculable distance'; so far, that every trace and memory of them is gone. There is no shadow of fear that these sins will ever be brought before us again. Even Satan cannot bring them back. And that is why you can know absolute cleansing and removal of guilt. Your sins are not just forgiven, they have been taken away!

And having removed our sins, God has credited the righteousness of His own Son to our account. God declares that we are now acceptable, we are family, we are His sons and daughters, adopted into the family through Christ. And He asserts that no charges will ever be brought against us. His wrath no longer rests upon us.

I realise that we don't always feel like sons and daughters of God, and I certainly realise that we don't always behave like sons and daughters. My children don't always share my outlook or my ways, but that doesn't make them any less my children. I am not accepted before God by performance, but by propitiation. Christ is the propitiation for my sins, and it is in His dealing with my sins, once and for all, that I find my acceptance with God.

Let me just say one thing. There is no sin that is excluded from that statement. There is no perversion so strange, no sin that you have committed so often that it is not covered by it. It is not like a domestic insurance policy in which some things are covered and some excluded. Everything is covered by this offering which our Priest has made, which is entirely acceptable to God.

Thirdly, we have freedom from guilt because of:

The position He now occupies

We saw in verse 12 that He is 'sat down at the right hand of God'. There is so much we can learn from that one phrase.

First of all, of course, *He's alive!* Having died in our place, God has raised Him from the dead. And Paul assures the Romans (Rom 4:25) that He was raised to life for our justification.

Secondly, the resurrection proclaims that *God is entirely satisfied with the work of Christ*. We know that when Christ cried 'Finished!' on that cross, it was His work, not His life, that was finished.

You know, if God hadn't raised Him publicly from the dead, we might have concluded that it had all failed; that bearing the punishment for the guilt of our sins had been too much for Him. But no, God raises Him bodily and publicly, and shows Him to be the conquering Saviour.

Having raised Him, Christ is now ascended to the right hand of God. Chapter 4 describes it like this: 'He has passed through the heavens' (4:14). It's another reference back to the Old Testament practice, when the high priest would enter once a year into the holiest of all with the blood of the sacrificed animal. He went to represent the people, to make atonement for their sins; and he would sprinkle the blood on the mercy seat. For the people waiting outside, there was just one all-important question: 'Is God going to accept this sacrifice? Will He accept the blood of the atonement?' And then they would hear the tinkling of the bells on the hem of the high priest's robe, and they would know he was coming out alive and all was well. His offering was acceptable.

Christ as our High Priest has entered into heaven, offering His own body and blood, and there He remains, seated at the right hand of God. The fact that He remains seated there is proof that His work is fully complete and absolutely acceptable by a holy God, and that in heaven He ever lives to make intercession for us. He is there at this very moment in time, at the right hand of the Father, proclaiming that He has borne my guilt and your guilt and all of its punishment. Do you know—His very presence there is making intercession for us?

Now, with all that in our minds, let's just sit back and enjoy verses 21 and 22. Let those words with that background flood your mind with peace and with confidence:

Since we have a great priest over the house of God, let us draw near to God with a sincere heart in full assurance of faith, having our hearts sprinkled to cleanse us—

—from what? From that which the Old Testament sacrifices could not touch:

—from a guilty conscience and having our bodies washed with pure water.

To any who are uncertain of their acceptance with God this evening comes the voice that brought encouragement to the soul of John Bunyan in that great book *Grace Abounding to the Chief of Sinners*:

Sinner, thou thinkest that because of thy sins and infirmities I cannot save thy soul, but, behold, My Son is beside Me and upon Him I am looking and not upon thee, and I will deal with thee according as I am pleased with Him.

Guilt is gone and cleansing is yours, because of the Priest who is ours, the price that He paid, and the position at the right hand of God that He now occupies.

The cleansing and power that is available to us

In verses 15 to 17, our writer takes us back to Jeremiah's prophecy of the new covenant, recorded in the thirty-first chapter of that prophecy. And, as F.F. Bruce comments, the new covenant, according to Jeremiah's prophecy, not only involved the implanting of God's laws in the hearts of His people, but also the will and the power to carry them out.

Praise God! Our message tonight goes further than cleansing. It goes further than freedom from guilt! There is *power* in our gospel. The new covenant is not imposed on man from the outside, it is not merely a law to be obeyed. It is written on our minds. It is placed into our hearts. There is spiritual desire implanted, there is enabling given through the indwelling Holy Spirit.

The gospel is more than 'Christ died for our sins and rose again for our justification'. I have been crucified with Christ and I no longer live, but Christ lives in me. Not only did Jesus die on the cross, bearing away all my sin; I died there also. Calvary gets rid of both the sin and the sinner.

Ron Dunn illustrates this in a quite daring way, which I'm going to adapt slightly. Suppose on your way home from this meeting you suddenly hear police sirens, and you follow the police cars to a supermarket. It's been robbed. Pushing your way through the gathering crowd you find the police inspector and you ask, 'Have you any idea who did it?' And he replies, 'Yes: we have evidence that Winston Churchill was the robber.'

'Impossible!' you say. 'I've got evidence that Churchill died long before the crime was ever committed.'

Do you realise that, in Christ, you actually died before you committed any of your sins? When the devil, the accuser, approaches God and charges me with sin, God merely looks up my record and says, 'No, impossible, it couldn't have been. He died two thousand years ago.'

It's a dangerous illustration, because I wouldn't like you to think that it lessens your responsibility for sin. But in a judicial sense it is true. Those sins will never be laid to my charge or to yours. We are crucified with Christ, and as Paul tells the Romans, that's a key factor in spiritual victory; to be daily taking that place of death with Christ and reckoning ourselves to be dead with Him.

And it's here that we begin to see the power of our gospel.

In Romans 6:14, Paul writes, 'Sin shall not be your master, because you are not under law, but under grace.' Now, imagine it: here's a slave in Paul's day, he's longing to be free from his master; but he hasn't got the resources to buy his freedom, and his master has no interest in granting it. The only way that bondage can ever be ended is by death. After his death, however much the master shouts and raves, the slave will not respond.

'We have died,' says Paul, 'to the mastery of sin. It no longer has dominion—it can shout and it can rage—but it no longer has dominion.'

Now, for that to be my personal experience, I know that a thousand times a day and maybe more I have to say to self, 'You are crucified! You may be still struggling to get off that cross, but by faith I am going to hammer those nails back in again today. Flesh, you are crucified!'

No to self, death to self; yes to the resurrection life within you. Crucified with Christ, but nevertheless Christ living in you. Cleansed tonight, freed from guilt and filled with the resurrection life of Christ; the presence in power of the Holy Spirit within you.

Now, just look, as I close, at how our section ends. All

that the Old Testament sacrifices could not do is done by this one sacrifice.

Verse 17: 'Their sins and their lawless acts I will remember no more.' That's removal, isn't it! Wiped even from the memory by God. Scripture tells us that our sins are nailed to the cross of His Son. They're dropped into the depths of the deepest oceans. And God says to you tonight, 'Your sins and your iniquities—as you turn from them and repent of them, I will remember them no more. I will not only forgive them, I will remove those sins, as far as the east is from the west.'

And verse 18: 'Where these have been forgiven, there is no longer any sacrifice for sin.'

> No blood, no altar now:
> The sacrifice is o'er;
> No flame, no smoke ascends on high,
> The lamb is slain no more.
> For richer blood has flowed from nobler veins,
> To cleanse the soul from sin and cleanse the reddest stain.

My brothers and sisters, that's my birthright, that's your birthright, as God's children. Don't allow Satan to rob you. Let's not leave it as theory or theology in a book, but let's go out and live in the good of these realities, for the glory of our risen Saviour. Amen!

1. See the address by Canon Keith Weston, p.159 of the present volume.

THE MASTER'S MEN

by Rev. Jim Graham

Mark 3:13–19

Throughout almost the whole of the third chapter of Mark, verdicts are passed on our Lord Jesus Christ, and reactions can be seen.

In verses 7 to 10, Jesus is regarded by the great crowd as *a miracle worker*. In verses 11 and 12, He's regarded as *the Messiah*: 'Whenever the evil spirits saw him, they fell down before him and cried out, "You are the Son of God." But he gave them strict orders not to tell who he was.' (It's very interesting that the dominion of darkness recognised who He was before His own disciples did. It took the disciples two-and-a-half years into His public ministry to recognise who He was. That came through the lips of Peter when he said, 'You are the Christ, the Son of the living God.' Actually it took them three years to call Jesus 'God', and that came from the most sceptical and the most doubting of all the disciples, where Thomas said, 'You are my Lord and my God.')

Then, in verses 20 and 21, Jesus is regarded as a madman, 'out of his mind'. The word is *existemi*, which means 'out of Himself', and that's how they regarded Him.

Then, in verses 22 to 30, Jesus is regarded as *evil*. In verse 22 the teachers of the law from Jerusalem say, 'He is possessed by Beelzebub', and in verses 23 to 30 Jesus' response is recorded.

And then, in verses 31 to 35, Jesus is regarded as simply *an ordinary man*: 'Then Jesus' mother and brothers arrived. Standing outside, they sent someone in to call him. A crowd was sitting around him, and they told him, "Your mother and brothers are outside looking for you." '

And they discover that Jesus is much more concerned about relationships than He is about relatives, although He is not unconcerned or irresponsible towards His relatives.

But you'll notice that I've left out a little cameo in verses 13 to 19, where Jesus' *lordship* is quite clearly demonstrated. There is power and authority in verse 13: 'Jesus went up into the hills and called to him those he wanted, and they came to him.' And the familiar list of disciples follows.

In these verses Jesus is regarded as *the master, the Lord*. For every time that the New Testament speaks of Jesus as Saviour, it speaks of Him twenty-nine times as Lord.

In Britain we have a struggle to appreciate the implication of saying that Jesus is Lord, because we only have a constitutional monarch. We know that the real power in the land does not lie in Buckingham Palace, but in Downing Street. So it's hard to grasp the biblical meaning of Jesus being Lord. It means giving up our right to a life of our own. It means surrendering our life in a quite radical way to Jesus as Lord and Saviour.

In a church magazine originating from the United States, the pastor wrote as follows: 'We have made a great mistake in the church by trying to get people to accept Jesus as Saviour. That is unscriptural. Never once does the Bible speak about getting people to *accept* Jesus as

Saviour. When we acknowledge Him as Lord, at that point He *becomes* our Saviour. Today the Lord is trying to impress upon us again the radical nature of being a Christian, and what it means in essence is putting our lives under the lordship of Christ.'

That's where we are on this evening here at Keswick. That's why I've turned to these few verses in the third chapter of Mark.

You see, Jesus needed to do two things.

First of all,

1. Jesus needed to ensure the future
That is why He gathered these disciples together.

One of the best-known legends about Jesus tells that when at last He went to heaven, after His passion, and the angelic host saw the evidences of the redemption that He had secured by His precious death on the cross, and as they recognised the cost of salvation, one of the angelic host said to Jesus, 'What provision have You made for the future?' Jesus called them over to the balustrade of heaven and they looked down to an upper room, and there they looked at eleven men who rejoiced that Christ was risen, but were still fearful and lacked courage. And Jesus said, 'I have made no other provision but that.'

And Jesus, in this little section, is calling together His disciples.

2. Jesus needed to extend His ministry
Secondly, Jesus was aware that He could only be in one place at one time during His incarnation, and He needed to extend the ministry that He had begun. And in Mark chapter 3 He's already thinking forward to that time when He'll have gone to the cross, when He'll have risen from the dead and when He'll have ascended to be with the Father in glory; and He would need a new body on earth.

And the difference between the Gospels and the Acts

of the Apostles is simply that Jesus has changed bodies. In the Gospels we see Him in His incarnate body—God become flesh. But in the Acts of the Apostles we see Him in His new body. That new body is the church after Jesus' ascension. There's a man in heaven tonight, and His name is Jesus. And He needs a new body on earth to declare the word of God and to demonstrate the works of God.

Revival will come in this land, ladies and gentlemen, not when churches are filled with people but when people are filled with the Holy Spirit and are living the Jesus-life in His power. And that's our calling as Christians.

In this passage, Jesus is calling together a new community and is making these early beginnings to extend His ministry.

There are three questions that I want to ask and attempt to answer tonight, and they come out of this passage that you have before you. The first is,

Why did Jesus choose the twelve?

In verse 14 Mark tells us there were two reasons.

1. For communion

The first reason is, 'that they might be with Him'. The Lord Jesus Christ is looking for communion with His people.

Very often as Christians we become extremely self-centred and we lay a great (and necessary) emphasis on our need of Christ. But in this passage we are reminded of His need of us; we need to be concerned about His desires and His needs. We have been created for God's sake. But God was not created. He is eternal. He is not there for our sake.

This often impresses me in the whole area of worship. We can become very self-centred in our approach and attitude, which are often determined by what *we* think, what *we* want, what *we* feel, the desires of *our* hearts. But in fact, biblically, worship is concerned about what *He* wants, what *He* is looking for; it is concerned with what will bless God and exalt Him.

So worship is only one of the ways in which we can recognise the needs of God's heart, that can be supplied out of our devotion and our response resulting from His relationship with us.

I know perfectly well that we need Jesus for pardon; there is salvation in no other. I know that we need Him in order to know what God is like; He and the Father are one, and Jesus said, 'He who has seen me has seen the Father.' I know that we need Jesus in order to know the power of the Holy Spirit; He is the one who communicates Him. I know that we need Jesus to pray for us, and there's a man in heaven who knows what it's like to be on earth, and He's praying for us tonight, interceding before the Father on our behalf. And I know that we need Jesus to prepare a place for us.

But I sense tonight that the Lord Jesus wants to say to us, 'Son, Daughter, I need you.' And that is why He appointed the Twelve. For communion.

2. *For commissioning*

Secondly, He chose them for commissioning them—that He might send them out to do two things: 'to preach and to have authority to drive out demons' (verses 14,15).

a. To declare His word

I sense, particularly as I move around this country, that there tends to be a loss of confidence in preaching. There's a great emphasis on worship, and I value that. There's a great emphasis on fellowship, and I covet that. There's a great emphasis on testimony and experience, and that's part of the on-going life of the church of Jesus Christ. But there needs also to be at the heart of the vibrant life of the church the declaration of the word of God, for it is God's word for all time, in every place, for all people. Jesus chose the twelve to declare the eternal, unchanging word of the kingdom.

But the second reason why He commissioned them was,

b. To have authority to drive out demons

They were commissioned firstly to declare God's word, but, secondly, to demonstrate God's power. Jesus is Lord, and we have authority delegated to us to confront the dominion of darkness.

It's one of the tragedies in the United Kingdom today that many Christians imagine that they're civilians, when in fact they're soldiers. We have persuaded ourselves that we are living in peace-time when in fact we are living in war-time. We are set against a subtle and a strong enemy who has devious tactics and who has an unrelenting strategy against the people of the living God. Modern people tend to discount his existence, but right at the heart of the inception of the ministry of Jesus we find that He sent them out 'to have authority to drive out demons'.

William Law says of Satan's relentless activity that 'He never slumbers, never is weary, never relents, never abandons hope. He deals his blows alike at childhood's weakness, youth's inexperience, manhood's strength and the totterings of age...As the spirit quits the tenement of clay, he still draws his bow with unrelenting rage.'

But Jesus who is Lord calls us to Himself, first of all for communion with Himself, and then to be commissioned by Him to declare His word and demonstrate His power.

Why did Jesus choose twelve rather than another number?

The second question is: why did Jesus choose twelve? Why not ten? Why not fifteen? Why not twenty-five?

The reason is simply that to the Jews twelve was a significant and a sacred number. Their nation had begun with one man who had twelve sons, who had twelve families, which became twelve tribes, which became one nation. And here Jesus is calling into being another twelve.

He could hardly have made a clearer statement by this action. He's saying that God needs a new people. That's why on Sunday we meet in a church rather than in a synagogue, why we celebrate on a Sunday rather than on a Saturday.

But there's an awesome reality contained in this. God can set His people aside. I've seen it happen in individuals. And God can set churches aside; I've seen that happen in Britain—churches that in the past have had a mighty, effective, relevant, powerful ministry no longer have. And He can set aside conferences, He can set aside conventions, and I see that happening in different parts of the world.

Let me try to illustrate it this way. Suppose you want to have a cup of water. You go to your cupboard and choose a glass. But you discover that by some chance the glass that you've selected hasn't been properly washed. So you're faced with two options: either you take the glass and rinse it out before you use it, or you set that glass aside and you go back to the cupboard and choose a clean glass.

In Mark 3:13–19, Jesus is choosing a new community of people who will declare His word and demonstrate His power under His authority. And perhaps the Lord is going to speak into your heart, or, if you're a church leader, into your church—just to see that you are moving on with God, that you're there where God is on the move today, fulfilling His current contemporary purposes, exalting His Son and bringing glory to His name.

That's why Jesus chose twelve men. The third question is:

Why did Jesus choose these twelve in particular?

One of our missionaries once gave me a sheet of paper. It was entitled 'A Memorandum', and read as follows:

To: Jesus, Son of Joseph, Woodcrafter's Shop, Nazareth.
From: The Jordan Management Consultants, Jerusalem.
The Subject: A Staff Aptitude Evaluation.

Thank you for submitting the resumes of the twelve men you have picked for management positions in your new organisation. All of them have now taken our battery of tests and we've not only run the results through our computer, but also arranged personal interviews for each of them with our psychologist and vocational aptitude consultant, bless him. It is the staff opinion that most of your nominees are lacking in background, education and vocational aptitude for the type of enterprise you are undertaking. They do not have the team concept. We would recommend that you continue your search for persons of experience in managerial ability and proven capability. Simon Peter is emotionally unstable and given to fits of temper. Andrew has absolutely no qualities of leadership. The two brothers James and John, the sons of Zebedee, place personal interest above company loyalty. Thomas demonstrates a questioning attitude that would tend to undermine morale. We feel that it's our duty to tell you that Matthew has been blacklisted by the Greater Jerusalem Better Business Bureau. James the son of Alphaeus and Thaddaeus definitely have radical leanings and they both registered a high score on the manic depressive scale. One of the candidates, however, shows great potential. He is a man of ability and resourcefulness, meets people well, has a keen business mind and has contact in high places. He is highly motivated, ambitious and innovative. We recommend Judas Iscariot as your controller and right-hand man. All the other profiles are self-explanatory. We wish you every success in your new venture.

So why did Jesus choose these twelve? Let me tell you. There were two reasons:

First of all, *because they were different from each other*. They were different politically, they were different educationally, they were different socially, they were different vocationally, they were different geographically (for eleven of them came from the north and one of them came from the south). Jesus chose them because they were different.

Secondly, *because they were 'anybodies'*. You might well ask the question, 'What did they have that others didn't have?' And the answer is, 'absolutely nothing'. They were neither 'somebodies' nor 'nobodies'. They were 'everybodies' and they were 'anybodies'.

And if God can do it through them, then God can do it through you and me; and I say to you that Jesus as Lord walks among us again tonight, and He calls us because He wants us. And because we recognise His lordship right across this tent, we respond.

In a few days we'll go down from this place, and we'll go down with the commission of Jesus ringing in our ears as He sends us back to whence we came, with a desire in our hearts to demonstrate to this nation—or wherever He has put us—that our God reigns and Jesus Christ is alive. It is for that purpose that we've come, and it is in that confidence that we'll go.

Ladies and gentlemen,

The world's great heart is aching, aching fiercely in the night;

And God alone can heal it and God alone give light.
And the men to bear that message and to speak the living
   word
Are you and I, my brothers, and all others who have heard.

God bless you.

SPIRITUAL DRYNESS

by Mr Victor Jack

Hosea 14:1–9, John 7:37–44

Is it possible that you've come to Keswick aware of real spiritual dryness in your heart? There was a time, perhaps, when your life was wonderfully enriched by the presence of Jesus; but tonight you're feeling somewhat impoverished, and you're experiencing barrenness in your soul instead of the fruitfulness you once knew of a life lived in fellowship with God. There's a numbness and a deadness there, instead of the freshness and the joy that once you knew. Your worship has become somewhat stilted and stale, and your service for God rather lethargic and mechanical. Prayer has become a grind and the Bible is no longer alive; and to read it has become a bit of a chore.

Maybe your experience tonight is summed up in the words of the old hymn:

Where is the blessedness I knew
When first I saw the Lord?
Where is the soul's refreshing view
Of Jesus and His word?

I'm convinced that there are people here tonight who

are feeling dry in spirit, but also have a real ache in their hearts to know what it is to be renewed afresh in the Holy Spirit.

If we're really honest we have to admit that it is easy to get out of vital touch with God. It isn't something that's necessarily deliberate. It can happen quite imperceptibly, almost without our realising it; a little bit like dry rot in the timbers of a well-established building.

How God grieved over the kind of spiritual decline that existed among His people in Hosea's day! Hosea uses two graphic pictures to illustrate how this spiritual decline had crept over the people of God.

Of Ephraim he writes, 'Foreigners sap his strength but he does not realise it' (Hos 7:9). And how easily we can find our spiritual vitality sapped because of the pressures of the life we live, or because we're becoming so immersed in society that we're losing our vital touch with God.

And then he uses another picture: 'His hair is sprinkled with grey, but he does not notice' (7:9) and 'despite all this he does not return to the Lord his God or search for him' (7:10).

Few of us go grey overnight. It's a slow process. The tragedy of Ephraim's condition was that he didn't realise it, he didn't notice it—the same kind of sad spiritual state that characterised Samson when he said, 'I'll go out as before,' and didn't know that the Lord had left him.

But I'm convinced that some of us here tonight do know of our sad spiritual condition. And we're crying out to God again to come and revisit us with the fullness of His Holy Spirit.

And so we turn to that beautiful illustration, or invitation, of Jesus in John 7 where He says 'on the last and greatest day of the Feast . . . 'If a man is thirsty, let him come to me and drink." And He went on to say, 'Streams of living water will flow from within him.'

It was the last day of the feast, when everything was moving towards a climax. There were thousands of pilgrims thronging Jerusalem. After several days of celebration, there was a very vivid ceremony when the high priest went down to the pool of Siloam with a golden vessel from the temple and filled it with water. A procession of people followed him back to the temple area, singing and waving their palm branches, and shouting verses from the prophet Isaiah: 'With joy shall you draw water from the wells of salvation.' The water was poured out on the altar, as the people sang through the great Hallel; and then there was a shout, a great shout: 'Oh give thanks to the Lord.'

And it would seem that in the deep silence that followed, Jesus was on His feet crying out like a herald: 'If a man is thirsty, let him come to me and drink.' At first it seems that Jesus is interrupting the proceedings, but in fact He was simply interpreting what was happening. The people were looking back some 1,400 years to that miraculous provision of water as they were travelling through the desert. And they were also looking forward with great anticipation to the time when the Messiah would come, bringing with him the water of salvation.

Jesus, in a very special way, was claiming to be the Messiah, standing among the people, claiming to meet the deeper spiritual needs of their personality.

And the same Lord Jesus is here tonight. And just as He could see the hearts of the people in Jerusalem that day, and knew that many of them were hungry and thirsty for God and yearning for the Messiah to come, so He can see into our hearts tonight; and He knows the dryness and the deadness that's there, but also the longing that we have for a fresh encounter with God.

And so we're going to look at causes of spiritual dryness, the cure for spiritual thirst and the consequences of spiritual renewal.

The causes of spiritual dryness

'Thirsty' is a word that Jesus used to underline the spiritual condition that we often go through as Christians. But we don't readily understand the word 'thirst' in Britain, because we're part of the privileged eighteen per cent of the world that has piped water in our homes.

In Jesus' day, however, people would often get lost in a dust storm, and their throats would become parched and their tongues like a board. Their whole bodies would begin to dehydrate as they cried out, desperate for water. So 'thirsty' is an appropriate word for Jesus to use, as some of us know only too well who have drifted from God but longed to find Him again.

It was the yearning of the psalmist: 'O God, you are my God, earnestly I seek you; my soul thirsts for you, my body longs for you, in a dry and weary land where there is no water' (Ps 63:1). We're told that our bodies are something like seventy per cent water, and they need regular intakes of liquid to replace natural losses. But because as Christians we're leaky vessels we need to come again and again to the Holy Spirit to know His filling in our lives.

The same *cri de coeur* is found in Psalm 143: 'I spread out my hands to you; my soul thirsts for you like a parched land' (Ps 143:6).

How is it that we get into this dry and arid condition? I will mention three causes out of many more.

There are spiritual causes. We've sinned against God, we've disobeyed Him, and so we've grieved the Holy Spirit. God's absence in our lives that we now feel is due to our sin. He has withdrawn the light and the joy of His presence, and we've lost our sense of fellowship with Him.

An unconfessed sin will always destroy our sense of well-being with God. So there are spiritual causes for dryness.

There are physical causes. We're overtired, we've stretched ourselves. This can be particularly true of missionaries and people involved in Christian work and church responsibilities. And what affects us physically has an impact upon us spiritually.

So when we are desperately, mentally and physically tired, and we're beginning to feel totally exhausted and dried up, it's then that we feel there's nothing left in our spiritual reservoirs. Unrelenting activity is a dangerous thing for any of us involved in Christian work; there can be a great deal of output, but very little input. And so we end up feeling desperately dry and barren in spirit.

And there are psychological causes. All sorts of pressures bear in on our minds and souls and drain us emotionally. There may be problems in your marriage, difficulties with the children at home, hassles at work, divisions in the church; and all these unresolved conflicts gnaw away at us subconsciously. And the enemy uses them as a tool against us so that we begin to turn in on ourselves in self-pity, or we turn outwards to others, in anger and frustration, instead of turning upwards in relief to God, who alone can pour in the refreshment of His Holy Spirit.

The cure for spiritual dryness

What then is the cure for spiritual dryness?

Jesus said it so simply and so beautifully that we could easily miss it: 'Come to Me and drink.' He is the fountain of living water.

Isn't it wonderful that He doesn't impose on us some heavy routine of religious disciplines such as characterise so many other cults and faiths? That He does not require us to make a superhuman spiritual effort to pull up our socks and do better? There *are* disciplines in the Christian life, but solutions based solely on human effort can only lead to greater despair and a growing sense of emptiness and lack of fulfilment.

But Jesus requires us to come to Him with nothing in our hands and only a confession of sin on our lips; because when we're empty and dry and spiritually barren, there is no-one else to whom we can go. As Peter said, 'Lord, to whom shall we go? You have the words of eternal life.'

But when we come to Jesus He requires of us an honest recognition of our true condition. We mustn't gloss over our failures and our weaknesses, or shrug off the promptings of the Holy Spirit as He touches our consciences and tells us all is not well. We live in a superficial age. We don't take God seriously, we are not honest with Him, and we're not honest with ourselves; so we don't allow Him to deal with us in a deep, life-transforming way. We must be really honest about our true condition, with genuine repentance.

'Take words with you,' says Hosea the prophet, 'and return to the Lord' (Hos 14:2). There's nothing vague or woolly here. Specific words of personal repentance, naming before God the weakness, the sin, the problem that has caused us to have lost our fellowship with Him. And then a true return to the Lord: Come back to Him. Turn your heart and your face toward Him, reaffirm your love for Him, open your life to Him and invite the Holy Spirit to come and fill you afresh again tonight.

And what a welcome you'll receive! As Hosea puts it (and these are God's words): 'I will heal their waywardness, I will love them freely' (14:4).

So the invitation of Jesus tonight is simply, 'Come to Me and drink; drink of My forgiving love, drink of My healing grace, drink of My renewing power.'

I'm reminded of the story of a tourist in America for the first time wanting to drink from a water fountain in a park. He couldn't see how to make it work. It had no tap or buttons to press. And he became very angry and frustrated.

He was about to turn away when somebody pointed out to him a little notice on the bottom of the fountain that simply said 'Stoop and drink'. So he did so, and discovered that an electronic eye detected his presence and all the water he needed came flowing out.

'Stoop and drink.' All we can do when we get into this low, empty, desperate condition is to come back to our Lord Jesus with our feelings of brokenness, emptiness, deadness and despair, and just kneel before Him and drink afresh of Him.

Many years ago I read some words in a book. I have never been able to discover their author.

> Upon the sandy shore an empty shell,
> Beyond the shell infinity of sea;
> Oh Saviour, I am like that empty shell,
> But Thou art the sea to me.
> A sweeping wave rides up the shore
> And lo! each dim recess, that coiled shell within,
> Is searched, is cleansed, is filled to overflow
> With water crystalline.
> Not to the shell is any glory then;
> All glory give we to the glorious sea
> And not to me is any glory when
> Thou overflowest me.
> Sweep over me, Thy shell, as low I lie;
> I yield me to the purpose of Thy will;
> Sweep up, oh Conquering Wave, and purify
> And with Thy fullness, fill.

Isn't that the prayer of your heart tonight? And Jesus uses the image of abundant water as an image of the ministry of the Holy Spirit: 'By this he meant the Spirit, whom those who believed in him were later to receive' (Jn 7:39). It illustrates the need to be filled and filled again with the Holy Spirit as the circumstances demand—because spiritual thirst is really a permanent Christian condition.

It's true, Jesus promised that if anyone came to Him and drank, He would relieve them of thirst. He did that initially for us, when we came to Him for salvation, and our thirst was quenched: but it breaks out again because we're weak and wayward, we sin and fail, and we need to come back and drink again.

All the tenses in this passage are in the present continuous tense: keep coming, keep drinking—because you'll keep getting thirsty. We will not cease to thirst until we get to heaven. In this life, we find great fulfilment in our Lord Jesus, but the foretaste that we have in Christ now makes us cry out for the full taste that we've yet to experience in heaven. We must 'keep on being filled', as Paul expresses it in Ephesians 5:18, if we translate his present imperative tense correctly.

Perhaps you need to find a quiet place to pray with somebody tonight, to ask God to fill you with His Holy Spirit. I thank God for the elderly gentleman who once encouraged me to get down on my knees with him and to invite the Holy Spirit to fill and to flood my life. But when we come to this point, there are always problems that seem to invade our minds and our spirits.

In our minds there are often doubts and fears—'Dare I really go this far?' And, sadly, because of the confusion and the controversy that rages around the ministry of God's gracious Holy Spirit, many are filled with suspicion and with fear, with unbelief and lack of faith. And so we quench the Holy Spirit, who wants to come and drench us with the blessings of God.

There may be a problem in our hearts also; sin may be blocking the channel, so that the Holy Spirit is grieved by our bitter attitudes and unforgiving spirit. Until that channel is cleared, the Holy Spirit cannot flow.

Or there may be a problem with our will—which is always the last citadel to be conquered; we're not really yielded to the Lord, so the Holy Spirit cannot flood our lives.

> I came to Jesus and I drank
> Of that life-giving stream;
> My thirst was quenched, my soul revived
> And now I live in Him.

We want that to be your testimony here at Keswick, but we have to come, I believe, to a specific point where we stoop and drink for ourselves, where we kneel and pray before the Lord Jesus, feeling broken, empty, longing afresh for the filling of His Spirit.

The consequences of spiritual renewal

When the Lord comes in all His power and fullness to refresh and renew somebody—all concepts contained in the final chapter of Hosea—'as the Scripture has said, streams of living water will flow from within him... By this he meant the Spirit' (Jn 7:38–39).

It's difficult to identify the Old Testament scripture to which Jesus was referring. But it may have been one of many beautiful passages in Isaiah, such as the promises 'I give water in the wilderness, rivers in the desert, to give drink to my chosen people' (43:20) and 'I will pour water on the thirsty land, and streams on the dry ground; I will pour out my Spirit on your offspring, and my blessing on your descendants' (44:3).

So Jesus in His invitation is depicting a thirsty traveller

who needs to come for a drink, and a thirsty land into which those who have been refreshed, revived and renewed need to go and take the living water to others.

If you travel to Israel, you'll see the results of long hot summers: hard ground, stunted bushes, dry river beds, and everything crying out for water. But wherever the fresh water of the sea of Galilee has been channelled, you will find lush growth and luscious fruit, even in the midst of desert conditions.

Our society today is like a desert, crying out for people who have first of all been filled by Jesus, and from whose lives there will be an overflow of Jesus towards others. And it would be a tragedy if we all came to Keswick just to strengthen ourselves. That is good, but from here we need to go out and be those rivers of living water in our community and in our homes.

What then are the consequences? There are at least three. First,

1. Freshness

God says, 'I will be like the dew to Israel' (Hos 14:5). The dew in Israel revived the flagging plants. Without it, vegetation would die in the Middle East. And God wants to revive us, renew us and refresh us. As Psalm 92 puts it, even in old age you can still bear fruit, you can still stay fresh and green (cf. Ps 92:14)!

And in Ephesians, the picture of somebody who's been filled with the Spirit is of somebody singing and making music in their hearts to the Lord; sparkling with praise (Eph 5:19). There's an aliveness and a freshness in Christ.

2. Fragrance

In Hosea 14:6 we read, 'His fragrance [will be] like a cedar of Lebanon.' The dew not only produces freshness, reviving flagging plants, but it also releases a beautiful fragrance into the morning air.

Near my office at home, climbing up an old tree, is a beautiful honeysuckle. On some summer evenings the air is impregnated with its beautiful scent. Don't we want that to happen in our lives? To be filled with the Holy Spirit, refreshed and alive in Christ, so that something of the beautiful life of Christ is released into our world?

Most perfumes we wear evaporate very quickly. But in 2 Corinthians 2:14, Paul talks about God through us spreading everywhere the fragrance of the knowledge of Christ. And only as we're filled by the Holy Spirit will there be an overflow of the beautiful life of Jesus.

Watchman Nee said, 'Christians should be like china tea; when they get into hot water, all the goodness should come out.' But often, alas, when we get into difficulties and hot water, much of the badness comes out.

When people come into contact with us, what do they pick up? The bad odour of our ugly nature? Or the beautiful aroma of the life of Christ?

Duncan Campbell has written, 'The greatest thing about us all is not what we say, it is not what we do; the greatest thing about us all is our unconscious influence and that unconscious influence impregnated with the life of Jesus.'

3. Fruitfulness
When the Holy Spirit fills our lives there's also a fruitfulness.

God says in this chapter, 'Your fruitfulness comes from Me; you will blossom like a lily, flourish like the grain, blossom like a vine' (cf. verses 5, 7, 8).

So the God who sends the dew which releases the fragrance now causes the fruit to grow; the fruit of the Spirit, which is love, joy, peace, patience, kindness, goodness, faithfulness, gentleness and self-control. God's heart is towards us tonight. He longs to bless us. As He said to Abraham, 'I will bless you and then make you a blessing.' He longs to fill us and then to flow through us.

Would to God tonight that our desire would be like Jacob's, who said, 'I will not let You go until, Lord, You bless me.' God waited forty years to hear that from Jacob; after years of independence and self-sufficiency.

How long has He waited for us? Will we hold on to God and say, 'I will not let You go until You bless me'?

God responded, and it says simply, 'He blessed him there,' and I believe that at Keswick He can bless us here.

So tonight find a quiet place, take a trusted friend with you, find somewhere to kneel and pray, and ask the Holy Spirit to fill your life afresh, to equip you for all that God has for you; so that there might be a new freshness, a new fragrance and a new fruitfulness in your life for His praise and glory. Amen.

THE HIDDEN FACE OF GOD

by Rev. Robert Amess

Isaiah 59:2

Would you turn with me, please, to Isaiah 59—initially the first two verses, although we will have a bird's-eye look at the whole chapter. You will see that in the New International Version this chapter is titled 'Sin, Confession and Redemption'.

Why does God hide?

Why is it the experience of the church, and of ourselves as individuals, that sometimes our God seems very distant and far away? The psalmist echoes our cry: 'Why, O Lord, do you stand far off? Why do you hide yourself in times of trouble?' (Ps 10:1).

Why does God hide? Why does it appear that He is hidden from the church in Britain? (I speak in general terms, for God is doing majestic and wonderful things around the world.) Why is it that revival does not come? Why is it that society does not seek the face of God? Why is it that quite clearly the vast majority of people have no concern for spiritual things? Why does God seem hidden to the believer?

For many of us, belief is easy but is belied by the facts.

For some it may possibly be make-believe. And I ask the question, are God's promises still true? Is the word of God to Joshua our promise too: 'I will never leave you nor forsake you' (Josh 1:5)? Then—where are You, my God? And the Lord Jesus Christ—is He yet the same? Is He still mighty to save? Those of us who had the privilege of being closely involved with the ministry of Billy Graham in recent months might say: 'Yes, He is mighty to save, but oh! that He would save more.'

Charles Wesley wrote of the Saviour:

> Thy name salvation is,
> Which now we come to prove;
> Thy name is life and health and peace
> And everlasting love.

Yet we might ask: then why don't You save more, my Christ? And is the Holy Spirit still active in power among us? We sing,

> His touch has still its ancient power,
> No word from Him can fruitless fall;

But where is that power? There is so much talk of it, but apparently so little demonstrable evidence of the gracious work of the Holy Spirit amongst us.

You say to me, 'Robert, you overstate the case.' And perhaps I do. 'Hyperbole,' you say, and I agree, but there is truth in what I say.

The truth stated

In verse 1 Isaiah sets forth the reality of divine power. 'The arm of the Lord' is an anthropomorphism. It's so gracious of God to give us words by which we can understand Him, and we understand 'the arm of the Lord': the mighty arm of God, who controls the universe, who is establishing His kingdom, whose name is still love.

But where are You, O God?

And the ear of the Lord—can He hear when I pray? Is He deaf to my need? Is He ignorant of my pain? Is He unmoved by my situation? Isaiah sets forth the facts of God's power. But why does God not listen?

The problem explained

In verse 2, Isaiah, having stated the truth concerning our God, explains the problem.

There is no loss of divine power to answer my need. My situation is not explained by divine negligence. God is still mighty to save, His long arm can still reach me, His strong arm can still lift me up and hold me close. As for His ear, 'Everyone who calls on the name of the Lord will be saved' (Joel 2:32).

No: the problem is not with God. The problem is with me. It is my sin that comes between my praying lips and His hearing ear, between my pressing need and His open hand.

The trouble is this, my friends. We will not have Him to reign over us. And, in the words of the Authorised Version, 'If we regard iniquity in our hearts, he will not hear us' (cf. Ps 66:18). Sin in the believer separates us from God.

Well, yes, of course; we are all agreed, sin is the problem. It's Monday night at Keswick and we always hear about sin in the believer at Keswick! You've heard it all before.

But, you see, having stated the situation, we must not leave it there. If I have overstated it, I have overstated it but a little. It is the gracious, if painful, work of the Holy Spirit to apply His word to every heart.

If you look at chapter 59, you will see that there are sins

laid out before us, which I would seek to apply to our
situation. Immediately those of you who are preachers
will say, 'Well, yes: but these are corporate sins, and this
is a word to the nation'—and you are right. But I must
remind you and emphasise the fact that corporate sin is
individual sin multiplied. The sin of modern evangelicalism is the corporate sin of its people.

Stained hands

So Isaiah the prophet speaks in verse 3 of 'stained hands'.

The psalmist asks, 'Who may ascend the hill of the
Lord? Who may stand in his holy place? He who has clean
hands and a pure heart' (Ps 24:3–4). Isaiah speaks of
stained hands: a people who touch what they should not
touch, who take what is not theirs, who handle what they
should leave alone; a people who hanker after that which
is trite, cheap and at best secondary.

I could tell you as a working pastor of some who would
not steal a postage stamp, but yet have stolen another
man's wife. I speak of those who hanker after things which
we would disregard, but yet which captivate the mind and
exhaust the spirit and harden the heart. We sit complacent
and say, 'This is of no relevance to me.' But—are you
sure? And are we not yet touching those things which we
would best leave alone?

I was brought up in an age when a doctrine of separation was taught. We used to speak of the strangest things!
Should Christians go to the cinema? Should girls wear
make-up? Those sort of questions. And it was so easy.

On one occasion my wife and I and our children went to
Eastbourne and up on to Beachy Head. My wife has a
terrible head for heights, and I'm a bit of a tease. I was
pretending to take pictures and walking backwards
towards the cliff; and the children were looking over the
edge in an exaggerated way. You know the kind of thing,
you've done it yourself. All of a sudden, my wife burst

into tears, and said 'Please! Stay away from the edge!' We knew that we had taken the joke too far.

Why is there a debate among Christians? Can a Christian do this, can a Christian do that, can a Christian do the other? If there is a doubt, stay away. For those who see their God are those who have clean hands.

Lying lips

In verses 3 and 4, Isaiah speaks of lying lips, that say what we ought not to say.

None of us would brazenly lie. Of course not. But nevertheless, among us there has been a familiarity with the things of God that has bred contempt. Some of us have become just a little too 'pally' with the Almighty. Some of us have made professions which are not true of our hearts and which we have no intention to carry out in our lives. Perhaps our God has become a little tired of those who mouth His name and do not honour it. Perhaps there is a credulity gap among us, between what we say and what we do; between the bold professions that we make and the little fruit that we see.

Injustice

Next, the prophet speaks of injustice, in verses 4 and 8 and 9–11. Justice, he says, is far from us, and righteousness does not reach us. And I must tell you that there are things that are being done in the name of Christ today that bring no glory to His name; wrongs that have been perpetrated and dressed up in divine jargon, which are really the selfish outworkings of wicked men. And injustice is rife amongst us.

Here you'll say, 'But you *do* exaggerate.'

But I tell you that in the purposes of God I walk in quite broad evangelical circles, and I hear of things that I wish I had not heard. And I have heard tell of things which bring no honour to Christ. And there are things with which even I have had to do, that make me lie awake at night and say that not even the world would have countenanced such things.

Violent behaviour

In the second half of verse 6 Isaiah speaks of violent behaviour. And 'evil deeds' are not unheard of among us. Murdering a name. Assassinating a ministry. We act as we should not act and, Isaiah says in this very powerful verse, we end up naked: 'Their cobwebs are useless for clothing; they cannot cover themselves with what they make.'

And all of these things, whether they be true in particular or general of you, have an effect. They will cause us to lose our peace with God. They will certainly cause us to lose peace with each other inevitably, and certainly to lose peace in ourselves.

There are many people today who are walking civil wars. We do not heed the word of the prophet, for we have 'healed the wounds of the people lightly, saying, 'Peace, peace,' when there is no peace' (Jer 6:14, 8:11).

The solution given

Thirdly, Isaiah gives us the solution. What are we to do about these things individually, and as the people of God?

Honest admission

Firstly, there must be honest admission. Look at verses 9 to 11: let me read them to you, for the Bible must speak for itself:

> So justice is far from us, and righteousness does not reach us. We look for light, but all is darkness; for brightness, but we walk in deep shadows. Like the blind we grope along the wall, feeling our way like men without eyes. At midday we stumble as if it were twilight; among the strong, we are like the dead.

We all growl like bears; we moan mournfully like doves. We look for justice, but find none; for deliverance, but it is far away.

Open confession
Secondly, there must be open confession.

Verses 12 to 15 read like a paraphrase of the old General Confession (I often go to Anglican churches, and when I say the Lord's Prayer I feel slightly conspicuous, because I say the old version!). Catch the same emphases in Isaiah, who tells us that the time has come when we must, openly and honestly, tell the Lord how it is.

Personal redemption
But I cannot leave it there, for Isaiah goes on to speak of personal redemption. Look at verse 20, and the glory of it all: "The Redeemer will come to Zion, to those in Jacob who repent of their sins,' declares the Lord.'

A general promise
'The Redeemer will come to Zion.' Turn over the page to Isaiah 64 for a moment. There we read of the longing of Isaiah—a longing which we mirror in our day—that God might do a great and wonderful thing among us as He has done before.

Verse 1: 'Oh, that you would rend the heavens and come down, that the mountains would tremble before you!'

Verse 3: 'For when you did awesome things that we did not expect, you came down, and the mountains trembled before you.'

Verse 12—I wish I could read the whole chapter!—'After all this, O Lord, will you hold yourself back? Will you keep silent and punish us beyond measure?'

Lord, do a great and glorious thing among us, by Your Spirit, for this nation!

A particular application

Isaiah speaks to Zion, then to individuals within Zion, 'to those in Jacob who repent from their sins, says the Lord'.

That is a word to you and to me. I did not mention that matter which God has laid upon your heart. I did not catalogue that sin which you know so full well. But you need no preacher to tell you, for you know it full well.

'To those in Jacob who repent of their sin.' Not sins in general—that is too easy—but that sin of which God is speaking to you now; that shortcoming of which you know full well, that matter which causes you to groan.

Repentance—and forgiveness. For in God is forgiveness, full and free.

> I know a fount where sins are washed away,
> I know a place where night is turned to day;
> Burdens are lifted,
> Blind eyes made to see;
> There's a wonder-working power
> In the blood of Calvary.

'Forgiven'—the most precious, the most wonderful word in the English language.

In one of my churches we had a girl who went away to university, and while she was at university she completely went off the rails. She entered into every sin that you could conceive of. When eventually she came home from university, she was broken. She was spiritually unwell, she was physically unwell. She came to see me one day, and it all came tumbling out. And she said, 'God will never forgive me.'

For weeks I spoke to her of forgiveness in Christ, full and free. She said, 'I cannot accept it. I cannot believe that that is for me.' Until eventually I told her, 'I know no more, I can tell you nothing else.' She would not accept forgiveness.

I said to God, 'Lord, You've got to help me. I can't do anything else, I can't say anything else, unless You say something and do something.'

She came to see me one day and I felt led by God to ask her to write everything that was troubling her on a piece of paper. She scribbled away for perhaps ten minutes, and when she had finished writing she handed over the piece of paper to me. And I said, 'No, that's nothing to do with me. That's between you and the Lord. But I want you to go through the list, item by item, and repent of each sin and ask God to forgive you. And while you pray, I will pray.'

Eventually, after some time, she handed me again the piece of paper, with a cloudy face. I took it and tore it up into as many pieces as I could. I walked down the corridor to the bathroom and flushed those bits of paper down the loo and came back, and her face was radiant.

'They're gone,' she said, 'they're gone.'

And by a simple parable she knew that her sins were forgiven.

> The dying thief rejoiced to see
> That fountain in his day,
> And there may I, though vile as he
> Wash all my sins away.

Is God hidden?

Jesus said, 'Blessed are the pure in heart, for they shall see God.' With repentance and faith, God is hidden no more. Praise His name! Amen.

ANGER, ALIEN OR ALLY?

by Rev. George Hoffman

Ephesians 4:26

The last film I produced before leaving Tear Fund was called *Man of Compassion*. It was a visual exposition of the way our Lord uses the word 'compassion' throughout the Gospels in His preaching and in His teaching.

In one rather harrowing locality, we were filming inside a Laotian refugee camp, high up to the north of Thailand on the border of Laos. There Ruth Nickerson of South-East Asian Outreach had been working as a language teacher for some years.

During a lengthy interview I reflected with her on the meaning of the word 'compassion'. Remembering some of her more nightmarish experiences on the border area, she said to me, 'You know, compassion isn't a sweet senti-mental thing.' And then, shaking her fist, she said, 'Some-times compassion is raw anger; I can't feel compassionate, but I do feel angry.'

We showed the film in Cambridge, and a Hebrew scholar at the university came to me after the discussion and said, 'Did you know that anger is one of the root words in Hebrew for "compassion"? It is one of the motivations for compassion.'

It was so helpful in that chance conversation to see that

the motivating force for so much of our Lord's compassion was anger.

Another 'chance conversation' was with my own doctor. Over the years I've been used to a variety of questions from doctors in the course of medical examinations, but I must confess I wasn't quite ready for the last one. I had the examination, and as the doctor was folding up his stethoscope in that rather enigmatic way that doctors have when they fold up stethoscopes and put them away and look rather thoughtfully at you, he said: 'How do you cope with anger?'

I didn't get much sleep that night. I lay awake a long time thinking, 'How *do* I cope with anger?'

I knew what the Bible meant when it said, 'Do not let the sun go down on your anger.' But what did it mean when it said, 'Be angry but do not sin'?

Well, how did Jesus cope with anger? When was He angry, and why? And what can I learn from His anger?

A book I have found helpful on the subject is called, significantly, *The Gospel of Anger*, written by Alistair Campbell. In his introduction, he says something that is at first reading rather shocking:

> The gospel of niceness has had such an effect on Christian groups that anger is constantly evaded, denied and thereby exacerbated.

But the conclusion he arrives at from that statement is quite fascinating:

> Faced by injustice, the contempt for other people, the affront of death, or just the petty frustrations of living with some people, those who fear or deny anger experience a gnawing guilt which drives them deeper into themselves and further away from the true cause of the anger.

So one of my concerns is to identify some of those true causes of anger, so that my anger is not without good cause.

Not surprisingly, Alistair Campbell draws attention to the anger of the Old Testament prophets. And if you read through them, you'll see many variations on a theme: they express their anger at religion without reality; at profession without practice, and such subjects as selfish indulgence at the expense of social justice.

But within these themes again and again you find them berating God's people for one continuing constant sin, the sin of hypocrisy. And it's not without significance that our Lord's angriest outburst is for that same offence.

In Matthew 23 Jesus denounces the religious community of His day as 'snakes and vipers', for being self-centred and self-righteous. He dismisses them as 'blind guides and blind fools'. One thing about Jesus, He didn't mince His words or conceal His anger. He scorches them for their superficiality and their distortion of religious ethics and social values. Seven times He denounces them as 'hypocrites', for professing one thing and practising another.

It's interesting to understand the background to that word 'hypocrites'. It comes from the Greek theatre of drama and tragedy. Often you will see on the proscenium two crossed masks and little ribbons hanging down. It was the symbol of the early theatre of drama and tragedy. The two masks represent sadness and happiness, with their upturned and downturned mouths.

And the *hupokrites* were the play-actors. They concealed their true emotion behind the mask, and the mask was to reflect the emotion that they wanted to communicate in the course of the play.

You see the meaning behind the word 'hypocrites'? Play-actors, people professing one thing with a mask, and hiding behind it to disguise another.' And our Lord had the greatest possible condemnation, and expressed His greatest display of anger, for them.

Reflecting on this, I thought of some words of C.S. Lewis: 'Perhaps the greatest tragedy in the Christian world today is the fact that we are just playing at being Christians.'

Hupokrites, play-actors.

And when I see how far short we fall in facing up to one of our particular social responsibilities, and our unwillingness to share realistically with the poorer countries of the world, I realise the relevance of C.S. Lewis's condemnation.

Over the years, I have to confess, I have been very angry when I've returned from the poorer countries of Africa and Asia and Latin America. I've been angry at our preoccupation with our standard of living, while for three-quarters of the world's population their only concern is whether they can stay alive. That's the division in the world today.

It's often said that the price of freedom is eternal vigilance. In another sense, I believe that the price of plenty, which you and I enjoy to the full, is that those of us who have it must plead for those who have to survive in poverty. And I believe that our Lord is angered by our sin of silence.

Simon and Garfunkel used to talk about 'The sounds of silence'. Maybe someone can write a song about 'The sins of silence'. Solon, the great Greek legislator, was once asked, 'When will justice be achieved in Athens?' He replied, 'When those who are not affected by the lack of it feel just as strongly as those who are.'

I was reminded of that afresh when I read recently what Pastor Niemöller wrote from a Nazi prison in his memoirs.

He was looking back over his experiences during the Nazi regime:

> In Germany the Nazis came first for the Socialists, but I didn't speak up because I wasn't a Socialist. Then they came for the Trade Unionists, but I didn't speak up because I wasn't a Trade Unionist. Then they came for the Jews, but I didn't speak up because I wasn't a Jew. And then they came for me, and by that time there was no-one left to speak up for me.[1]

The sins of silence. Remember the question that Cain put to God. Remember his attempt to cover his guilt for killing his brother. 'Am I my brother's keeper?' The unequivocal answer that God gave him was: 'Yes. Yes, you *are* your brother's keeper, because he *is* your brother.'

That's at the heart of my responsibility. That's why I have to recognise my responsibility, living within a society and sharing the responsibility for the corporate sins of that society. If I don't speak out then I am condoning something by silence.

Now in John 2:12–16 I want you to notice the cause of another well-known display of our Lord's anger.

He literally whipped the traders off the premises. He saw red, as it were, at the misuse of religious means which were being used for personal ends, for personal profit and for personal well-being. That's what lies at the heart of the cleansing of the temple.

I have a similar reaction when I return from the refugee camps of Ethiopia; from an earthquake in Central America, from the slums of Calcutta, and I see the so-called 'Prosperity Gospel' being espoused and promoted.

Don't think it's not happening in your churches. Through our Christian periodicals and Press and in other ways, it's being subtly introduced in a variety of forms. The 'Prosperity Gospel'—crudely described by somebody as 'Name it, claim it, frame it!' Chuck Smith said to me the other day, 'Well, we put it slightly differently in America. "Blab it and grab it!" '

One exponent of this particular philosophy puts it like this: 'Through visualisation and dreaming you can incubate your future and hatch the results.'

What a glorious golden egg! For my welfare, for my well-being!

Such teaching has confused sincere Christians into imagining that faith is a force which makes things happen because they believe.

'Thus faith is not placed in God, but it becomes a power directed at God focused upon Him, so that He will do for us what we want Him to do.'

But that's not faith! It's a devilish manipulation.

You see, like the traders in the temple, the end has been forgotten, and the means has become merely a medium for obtaining selfish ends, instead of worshipping God.

Isn't this the reversed religion that Paul speaks about in Romans 1—when we worship the creature rather than the Creator, and God merely becomes a means to an end to achieve our desires?

Isn't it a reflection, to some extent, of our selfish preoccupation with our trivial pursuits? It was summed up for me by a caption that I once saw in a shop window coming through Amsterdam airport: 'I have high ideals, I want to make the world a better place for me to live in.'

Those are the kind of ideals that make me angry, and I see them reflected so often in our church values, our church budgets, our church goals and objectives, our church AGM's and our church meetings. We want to make the world, the church, this place, a better place for *us* to live in. And these are the kind of ideals, spoken or unspoken, that make God angry.

Recently I was travelling up from the south coast and stopped at Clapham Common in London for a few minutes. I was reminded of a group of angry men who used to meet there regularly at the end of the eighteenth century. Five of them were Members of Parliament, all thirty of the group lived close to Clapham Common, and they were card-carrying, Bible-believing, evangelical Christians. They became known as The Clapham Group.

Commenting upon the impact they made upon our country, Charles Colson says in *Kingdoms in Conflict*: 'Derisively labelled "The Saints", they bore the name gladly, considering such distinction a welcome reminder of their commitment not to political popularity but to biblical justice and righteousness.'

Again, they were a group of men who were sustained by compassionate anger to change society in the name and for the sake of our Lord Jesus Christ.

Now, among the Clapham Sect was a man who was young in years and young in faith. Soon after his conversion, he wrote in his diary these words:

> As soon as ever I had arrived thus far in my investigation of the slave trade, so enormously dreadful, so irredeemable did its wickedness appear, that my own mind was completely made up for its abolition.

Later, in 1791, he stood up in Parliament and said, 'Never, never will we desist until we extinguish every trace of this bloody traffic on which our posterity, looking back to the history of these enlightened times, will scarce believe that it has been suffered to exist so long a disgrace and a dishonour to this country.'

That angry young man was, of course, William Wilberforce. And that God-given anger sustained him for nearly thirty years of battle within the House of Commons, until slavery was finally abolished throughout the British Empire in 1833.

A few weeks after that magnificent achievement, he died. And at Wilberforce's funeral in Westminster Abbey was another young Bible-believing, card-carrying evangelical, another Member of Parliament. He was arguably the greatest social reformer that this country has ever produced. Besides being, in every sense of the word, a man of God, Ashley Cooper—Lord Shaftesbury—was a man of anger. Read his biographies. And this God-given anger was aroused by the conditions here in our country then that are similar to the hovels of Haiti and the barrios of Brazil now.

We can thank God for such men who pioneered social reform in our communities. But was this God-given anger that enabled him to accomplish the most astonishing achievements in his lifetime. It's a mind-blowing exercise just to list the organisations and associations that he established or promoted in his anger. The NSPCC, The Association in Aid of the Deaf and the Dumb, The Hospital and Home for the Incurables, John Groom's Association for the Disabled, The YMCA, The YWCA, The Baptist Missionary Society, The South American Missionary Society, The London City Mission, The Railway Mission, The Seamen's Mission, The Open Air Mission and The Church Pastoral Aid Society.

(The streets of Keswick would be empty during Convention week if it hadn't been for Shaftesbury!) And all of these activities were accomplished voluntarily, in his spare time! Through his political career, Shaftesbury introduced and fought for reformation at a social level that has affected every sector of our society—in factories, in mines, in hospitals, in prisons, in education and in commerce. He championed the cause of women and all who were distressed or disabled, ostracised or oppressed.

These were the causes for his anger which gave his anger a right cause. His anger was part of his Christian motivation for his compassion. And his anger was sublimated into action against the very object of his anger.

One final incident in the life of Jesus. I've been thinking about it recently with this theme in mind. It's found in Mark 3: an incident in the synagogue. It's a classic illustration of religious cant, which is nothing more than a devious ploy to achieve a dubious end.

There's a handicapped man with a crippled hand, but he's ignored. That's the first thing to notice: the man's need is ignored by the religious leaders. They don't even see him. They're so blinded by their undisguised attempts to discredit Jesus anyhow, by any means. That's a frightening kind of blindness.

In the second verse of Mark 3 we read, 'Some of them were looking for a reason to accuse Jesus, so they watched him closely to see if he would heal him on the Sabbath.'

So, angrily, He rounds them and He asks, 'Which is lawful on the Sabbath: to do good or to do evil, to save life or to kill?' And then, as is so often the case, we read, 'They remained silent.'

Do you remain silent tonight?

And then, before healing the man, we read that '[Jesus] looked around at them in anger and [was] deeply distressed at their stubborn hearts.'

I wonder if Jesus looks around at us again tonight in anger—deeply distressed at my stubborn heart, at your stubborn heart? Stubbornness for not seeing what He wants us to see. Stubbornness, blindness, for not sharing what He wants us to share, for not doing what He wants us to do. The stubbornness of blindness. The blindness of stubbornness.

Canon Guy King was a well-known Keswick speaker. In his commentary on Ephesians 4:26—that verse I

quoted at the beginning—'Be angry but do not sin'—
Canon King writes this: 'If our blood does not boil sometimes in the presence of cruelty, of injustice, of meanness,
of hypocrisy, there is at least one Christ-like quality missing from our spiritual make-up.'

That quality Martin Luther called 'the anger of love',
'one that wishes no-one any evil. One that is friendly to
the sinner. One that is hostile to the sin.' May God, then,
grant that this Christ-like quality might not be missing
from our spiritual make-up.

May God grant us the anger of love.

1. This was a passage with which Pastor Niemöller concluded many of his
post-war addresses.

FORGIVE AS WE FORGIVE

by Rev. Philip Hacking

Matthew 18:21–3

Aren't you glad the apostle Peter was one of those men who spoke his mind? I am. While the other disciples thought things, Peter said things. He was a blunt man. And he always echoed what other people were thinking.

It often happened. For example, when the rich young ruler was there, and they were all feeling a little bit cross because, after all, he'd turned his back on Jesus, and he was obviously a wealthy man. And Peter says, 'Lord, we've left everything and followed You. What will we get?' And out comes some lovely teaching by Jesus about the blessings that we receive when we're prepared to put Him first.

Or there was the moment when, in the Acts of the Apostles, Peter was on the rooftop having a snooze, and he had a vision of unclean animals and a voice saying, 'Rise, Peter, kill and eat.' Peter said 'No, Lord, I've never eaten anything common or unclean.' The message came: 'What God has cleansed, don't call common.' And out of that vision came the expansion of the gospel to the Gentile world.

Oh yes, thank God, Peter was honest enough to ask his questions.

The opening verses of Matthew 18, up to verse 20, are full of terrific, demanding teaching about discipleship.

He talks about being humble; in the first few verses, about being like a child. He talks, from verse 7, about the demands of living a pure life—'if your hand offends you, cut it off'—and in verses 10–14, about going out to seek the lost. And then—and this is the crunch!—our Lord begins to talk in verse 15 onwards about how to be reconciled to your brother: how to live a life of forgiveness.

Suddenly Peter blurts out, 'Lord, how many times shall I forgive my brother when he sins against me? Seven times?' He thought that was marvellously magnanimous! He probably knew the Old Testament passage where Job speaks about God forgiving twice, and even three times; and seven was a perfect number.

The answer comes back, 'Not seven times; seventy times seven' (or you may have a verse with 'seventy-seven times'; the Greek's not clear and it doesn't matter, for it's not a mathematical figure). Our Lord is saying, 'Go on and on and on.' Because, you see, the forgiveness of the cross goes on and on and on.

If you want a biblical background to this 'seventy times seven', it's way back in Genesis when a man called Lamech said this: 'Cain has been avenged seven times, Lamech seventy-seven times' (or 'seventy times seven'), Genesis 4:24. And that is what's happening in our world today. We inject vengeance, we want to get our own back.

But the message of the cross, the challenge for Christians, is to receive forgiveness and to demonstrate they receive forgiveness by being forgiving. For our Lord makes Himself desperately clear.

Just look at the end of the chapter: 'This is how my heavenly Father will treat each of you unless you forgive your brother from your heart' If we do not forgive, He would say, it is proof that we have never been forgiven, or that we have gone away from the reality of the cross.

Now, Keswick is all to do with practical holiness. It builds on a doctrinal foundation to which it is vital we hold on. 'But,' says Jesus in this very stirring parable, 'unless you forgive others, you really haven't been forgiven.' You must come back to the foot of that cross, for the demonstration that you are a forgiven sinner is that you are a forgiving sinner.

So let us look at this parable.

May I say one thing about parables? They aren't meant to be doctrinally transparent statements. They're stories. But they are very telling stories. And the parable before us keeps focusing in on that message of the cross.

There are three instalments, and the first is,

1. Forgiveness offered (verses 23–27)

a) The debt calculated

The picture of God as a King, and His servants as those who have to render an account, is fairly common in Scripture. The Bible is quite clear that all of us, individually, without anybody to help us will stand before the judgement seat; and we'll tell Him what we've done.

So here's a man who renders an account. 'He owed ten thousand talents.' Whether you translate it into pounds or dollars, it's a silly sum. It's a ridiculous sum. It's a sum you cannot calculate. It is saying to all of us, we owe God a debt that never ever, ever can we pay.

Our Lord has another story about two people who owed a debt. One five hundred, one fifty. Which would be the happier of the two when he'd been forgiven? The one who owed the most, of course.

And here's the challenge to us. There are some of us who have almost forgotten what a debt we have been forgiven.

I am more conscious of debts that I owe to God that I have not paid. The General Confession of the 1662 Prayer Book talks about the things we've done which we ought not to have done. And, yes, I can always think of those. But even more I must confess to having left undone those things which I ought to have done.

What debt do you owe to God?

You owe Him a debt of love. Do you love Him with all your heart, soul, mind and strength?

You owe Him a debt of service, a debt of prayer. Do you realise that prayerlessness is sin? 'God forbid that I should sin against the Lord in ceasing to pray.' Are you to be found with the people praying in your church? Or do you believe in it sincerely, but when it comes to the pinch you're never there?

You owe Him a debt to evangelise. 'Go and make disciples.'

All these are what we owe Him, so if we are not doing them we are in debt to God.

b) A debt cancelled

In verse 25, the master orders the man to be sold. That was reasonable by Old Testament law. He was trying to see whether the man had any sense of penitence before he was ready to forgive. I suspect he was always planning that he might forgive him, but here's the law.

The servant fell down on his knees saying, 'Be patient, and I will pay back everything.'

Might I say two things. Firstly, I hope we all remember that that's where every single one of us must always be. Billy Graham often tells a story of the man who said, 'Dr Graham, I don't want mercy, I want justice.' And Billy reminded him that not only for him, but for all of us, that if we get justice, we go to hell. Let's be quite clear: that's what I deserve. That's what justice is. Should I say to God, 'Give me my just rewards,' so be it. I don't care who you are, that's what you deserve. So all of us have to be on our knees.

I'm also intrigued by this man's optimism: 'Be patient with me and I will pay back everything.' I'm sure other ministers share my experience. The number of people who have been round to try to get money out of me! They're always going to pay me back. I'm still waiting for the first one to pay me back. One day he will, but I've never found one that does!

And here is this Micawber-like optimism—'I will pay back everything.' Really? Millions of pounds? You see, it's the innate sense in all of us that we want, if we can, to earn our freedom. We want to be different. 'The cross is needed for some people, but I want to go my way, I want to earn it, I want to get in my own way.'

There are people who seem determined to say, 'You can open the door wide—Jesus on the cross—but You needn't have bothered for me, I'll get there my own way. I may have gone through that door when I was saved thirty years ago, but now, you see, my kind of living is my own way...I am paying You back, Master. I am doing it my own way.'

And they forget that it's always all of grace. And so comes the gospel picture in verse 27, when the servant's master took pity on him. It's a strong word, used also about the Samaritan who was 'moved with compassion' when he had every excuse for not touching the injured Jew. Here is father, moved with love and with pity, and because he's moved with pity—please note the phrase (verse 27)—'he cancelled the debt'.

Oh, I wish I could get home to you what that really means. The tremendous cost of the cross. Isn't it so simple to say it? I mean, if you owed me £500, and I—being the sort of man I wish I were—said to you, 'Don't worry, forget it,' it wouldn't be forgetting it. It would be me paying that £500. And when the master in the story said, 'Forget the millions of dollars, forget that big sum,' who was paying it? He was.

Please, it's not that God said, 'All right, I'll forgive you, I'll let you off.' Some say that it's easy for God. No, it isn't. It cost Him His Son. He was in heaven and He heard His Son cry, 'My God, my God, why did You forsake Me?'

Have you entered into that? Some of you here will know what it is to go through the agony of seeing a child sick, dying maybe, but you can't do anything to help. And have you gone into the eternal mind? 'My God, My God, why?' And God had to let Him die. Unlike Abraham with Isaac, there was no last minute reprieve. The knife went in. That was God paying the price. It was Jesus paying the price—the Son of God—because He was God and man.

And, incidentally, the moment you diminish the deity of Jesus, the moment He's less than God, you've robbed the cross of all its meaning. Stand firm for Christian truth! It was the eternal Son of God who was made sin for us. And because of that the debt has been cancelled. There are some lovely words in the Old Testament. He has cast our sins into the depth of the sea (Mic 7:19); 'As far as the east is from the west, so far has he put our transgressions from us' (Ps 103:12).

When I was a student, I lived for a year with a very godly couple, and during that year I decided God was calling me to the ministry. My landlord was not an Anglican. I think he was rather bemused by this student who was going to be an Anglican clergyman, so he loved to ask me conundrums from Scripture. Do you know people like that, who love to ask you awkward questions? And every time, I failed miserably. He shook his head at these awful Anglican ordinands who were so bad on Scripture.

One of his questions, I remember, was, 'Tell me, Philip, why does the Psalm say 'as far as the east is from the west' and not 'as far as the north is from the south'? Now, of course, you all know the answer. I didn't know it then. I said, 'I give up.'

'Well,' he said, 'it's fairly obvious really, but I'll just explain it to you. You see, there is a North Pole and there is a South Pole and you can measure the distance. But where is west and where is east?' Some of you are nodding. I'm not sure the Psalmist ever knew that that was the interpretation, but never mind!

Behind my landlord's conundrum lay a great truth. It is such a distance that it is immeasurable. Our sins are gone for ever. And if you want to be even clearer, take Colossians 2:14, where Paul, throwing metaphors together, says that on the cross our sins were cancelled, torn up, nailed to the cross—gone. Now, because they're gone, you and I are completely, utterly forgiven. Not because of our worthiness, not because of our zeal in the Lord's service, but simply because of His grace. Hold on to that when you get guilt feelings, when Satan tempts you to despair!

But I want to take it further. There's a man being forgiven a tremendous debt. That's the first instalment. Jesus is saying, 'The debt's been cancelled. I have paid the price, your sins are gone, I will remember them no more. Now, forgive. And if you don't forgive, I don't believe that you've accepted My forgiveness.'

2. Forgiveness refused (verses 28–30)

If we'd not known human nature, we might have said that this story goes over the top. How could anybody, forgiven like that, go out from that and find a friend who only owed him a few pence and not forgive him?

Oh yes? Have you never broken bread and gone out from a church building and still refused to speak to somebody else who broke bread with you? Dare I say to you,

you are demonstrating by that very fact that you haven't grasped what it means to have been forgiven, you have forgotten what it means. How dare we refuse forgiveness for somebody who only owes me a trifle, when God has forgiven me all that debt?

Indeed, dare I say to God: 'Forgive me Lord, in the way I do not forgive'—where would we be if He answered that prayer?

And I want to say, this is not only an opportunity given but an opportunity lost. For when the person fell at his knees and begged him 'be patient with me, I'll pay you back' (verse 29), he refused and had him thrown into prison. Don't you see that here was a wonderful opportunity for the gospel ministry to be exercised? Here was a chance to show that he'd been changed.

The strange thing is, he had forgotten that he had been forgiven. Paul says, in Galatians 6, that we should restore the penitent sinner, always remembering that we too are sinners, lest we also be tempted. You find the same in Titus 3:2–3, where we're reminded that we must remember that we were foolish, disobedient, deceived and enslaved by passions and pleasures. We've been that way.

Do you remember that remarkable passage in 2 Samuel 12:5? Nathan wants to drive home to David the enormity of his sin, so he tells David a story. It's the story of a man who was rich and had plenty of things to offer, and a poor man who had only one ewe lamb. And the rich man didn't take of his own to feed his guest, he took the poor man's one ewe lamb, and took that to feed his guest.

And, as the story went on, David, it says, was indignant and David said, 'As surely as God lives, that man must die.' But he was signing his own death warrant. He was talking about himself and he didn't know it. What had he just done? He'd sent Uriah to his death, he'd committed adultery with his wife, and—I always think the greatest, most awful sin of all—he'd traded on Uriah's loyalty. He'd actually put into Uriah's hands the letter which said, 'Please put Uriah into the heat of the battle so that he'll die.' David knew that Uriah would never open that letter. His loyalty was absolutely clear. It's possible to sing 'The Lord is my shepherd' and yet not hear God saying, 'You are the man, you are the woman.'

You see what happened to David was that he didn't recognise himself; and the trouble about this man, when he saw this fellow doing an action-replay of where he'd been only hours before, he didn't see the connection, and missed the opportunity to forgive.

If we believe this message of complete forgiveness, if we really believe that Jesus on the cross paid the penalty, we need to be freed from the bondage of not being able to forgive. I would be surprised if God were not speaking to some, maybe many, in a very personal and practical way, 'Do you mean it? Do you believe it? Then go out and live it.'

You cannot preach the cross from the pulpit if you don't live it out in the pew. There is no point telling the world that He's died and it's finished and we're reconciled, when everything about our relationship shouts the opposite.

Now, here's my last little instalment.

3. Forgiveness withheld

Forgiveness offered, forgiveness refused—and forgiveness withheld.

Don't you find the last bit very strange? Often our Lord, when telling a parable, has a punch at the end. The sting's in the tail.

Don't you think, at the end, that the master ought to have forgiven the servant yet again? After all, hadn't Jesus said you must go on forgiving and forgiving and forgiving? So shouldn't the master have forgiven the man over again? Yet, in verse 34, he's handed over to be tortured until he's paid back all he owes, and Jesus hammers the point home in verse 35.

This speaks about God's judgement and God's justice.

The servants—his fellow-servants—were indignant. The world knows that Christians should forgive, so the message comes back to the master. And the master says to the servant, 'All right, if you want it on those terms, you may have it.'

Judgement is without mercy for those who show no mercy (Jas 2:13). What is God's justice? Here is our Lord's very solemn word. What He is saying is that God's love and forgiveness has a limit. Yes, that's what He's saying.

I meet people who want to tell me, 'Well, of course, God is love, and because God is love, love must vanquish everything; therefore, everyone must eventually arrive at heaven. God cannot send anybody to hell. He must have everybody in heaven and, therefore, ultimately God's love must triumph.'

But that's completely contrary to New Testament teaching. He's done everything in His love. He's paid the debt on the cross. He's gone all the way for us. But we still have the possibility of rejecting it. And if we do turn our back on that love, then there is only solemn justice.

We may say we believe the great truth of the atonement. But do we prove it by our attitude to Him and to others? Paul says, 'Forgive, because you've been forgiven; forgive as you've been forgiven' (Eph 4:32). So the demonstration that I really believe is not that I mouth the words of a hymn, nor that I sign forms at an evangelistic rally; the proof that I really mean it is that my life is changed. 'By their fruits ye shall know them.' So when Christians live forgiving lives, we know they are different;

and if they refuse to forgive, we do not know they are different.

These are solemn words, as I end. Yet at the same time they could be tremendously liberating words. What our Lord wants to say to all of us tonight is: 'I've forgiven you. In the light of that forgiveness, forgive yourself and forgive each other.'

I finish with the story of the woman taken in adultery. Do you remember? They said to Him, 'Shall she be stoned because of her sin? Shall we do what the law says?' And Jesus said, 'Go on, let the one who's without sin cast the first stone.'

Friends, some Christians become very legalistic. Some of us are very good at throwing stones. Because we care about moral standards we throw stones like nobody's business. Our Lord is saying, 'All right, would you dare roll the boulder on any of these people? Have you got a right to do it?'

And everyone went out, the woman turned to Jesus, and He said, 'Is there nobody here to condemn you?'

'No, Lord.'

Do you remember His great words? 'Neither do I condemn you. Go and sin no more.'

Never say one without the other. They must both be held together. He did not just say, 'Neither do I condemn you,' full stop. He did not just say, 'You are forgiven.' He said, 'Neither do I condemn you; go and sin no more.' And in the light of her forgiveness was the motivation for a new life.

I hear Jesus saying on that cross, 'Father, forgive them.' And when you've really been forgiven, you've got all the motivation in the world to go and sin no more, and you've got all the motivation in the world to go out to a world of need and say—not by your words so much as by your actions—'Neither do I condemn you, go and sin no more.'

That isn't treating sin lightly. How could you do that when it cost Jesus His life-blood? But it's treating forgiveness seriously. And there may be people tonight who are still bound by the law and by guilt. Or you're bound by bitterness and prejudice and unwillingness to forgive. Until those fetters fall, you'll never know the joy of the freedom of the gospel and the fullness of the Spirit.

Have you been forgiven? Are you forgiving? Will you make your response to the Lord? If you feel it would help to pray with one of us, we'd be delighted, because we want you to enter into the joy of His forgiveness.

VITAL QUESTIONS

by Rev. Chuck Smith

Romans 8:31–39

Surely one of the most important choices that all of us make in life is: 'What will be the master of my life? The flesh, or the spirit?'

Paul tells us that there is a warfare going on, of my flesh against my spirit. All of us experience that warfare, and all of us must make our choice about who will rule us. Whether Christ is to be the Lord of my life or not is something that I determine by choice. And what every one of us needs to recognise is that our eternal destiny depends upon the choice that we make.

I have talked many times to people who are reluctant to make the choice of Jesus Christ as Lord. And when you seek to ferret out the reason for their reluctance, you find that they have looked at the Christian life, they have seen others living it and they have admired it. In fact, they have often thought, 'I am not happy or satisfied with this life that I am living. I know that I am wrong. I am going to change. I am going to be a better person.'

And they have sought to be a better person; they have sought to give up some of the shackles and habits of the world. And they have discovered a total inadequacy. They haven't been able to do it. So they assume that they cannot live the Christian life because they have tried and failed, and so many times, for that reason, they do not surrender to the lordship of Jesus Christ—not realising that it's impossible to live the Christian life without the lordship of Jesus Christ. I cannot live for the Lord apart from the empowering of the Holy Spirit.

Jesus said to His disciples just before His ascension: 'But you will receive power.' I like the Greek word—*dunamis*. A couple of English words are derived from it— one is 'dynamite', and that's the one usually quoted in the commentaries.

There is another word—*dynamic*. It comes from that same Greek word. I prefer *dynamic* to *dynamite*. I've seen too many Christians who are blowing up! I'd rather see that drive and power, the *dynamics* of the Spirit. 'You will receive the dynamics—the power—when the Holy Spirit comes upon you, and you shall be witnesses unto Me; both in Jerusalem, Judaea, Samaria, and unto the uttermost parts of the earth.'

The dynamic—that power—is imparted to me when I surrender my life to the lordship of Jesus Christ.

I'm so glad of that day when I came to the place where I had enough sense to realise that I was doing a poor job trying to determine my own destiny and guide my own future and turned it over to Him. I placed my future in His hands, and He began His work in me. There are some wonderful things that I discovered when I surrendered to the lordship of Jesus Christ.

But I wasn't the first one to discover them. Paul discovered them and he wrote to the Romans about them. In chapter 8, Paul asked a series of questions and gave answers—questions that deal with the life that is surrendered to the lordship of Jesus Christ.

As I look at my relationship to Him today, these are

some of what you might call the 'fringe benefits' of following Jesus, allowing Him to be the Lord of our lives.

'If God be for us, who can be against us?'

I found that when I surrendered my life to the lordship of Jesus Christ, there was now a power with me, in me, that was greater than all the forces or powers of the world that I had or could face. 'Greater is he that is in you, than he that is in the world' (1 Jn 4:4). I no longer had to be defeated by my flesh and by that flesh-life. I no longer had to be a slave or a servant to sin. God was now for me. His strength and power were imparted to me and I could live a life of victory over the powers of darkness and sin. And what a glorious thing it is to know that God is for you!

For many years, growing up in Sunday School, I developed a wrong concept of God. Somehow I felt that God was against me. I was conscious of my failures and weaknesses. I would promise and vow to God that I would live a better life, and then I would fail. I would fall back into the same old rut. I was certain that God was as disappointed with me as I was with myself, and I really thought that He was just waiting for me to make mistakes so He come down on me in judgement.

My little grandson William came home from Sunday School one day, and he said to his father, who is a minister, 'Daddy, is God watching me?' And my son said, 'William, why do you ask?' He said, 'Well, my Sunday School teacher today told me that God was watching me. I want to know, is God watching me?'

My son asked, 'William, why did your teacher tell you that?' 'Oh,' he said, 'I was pulling the hair of the girl that was sitting in front of me...But I want to know, Daddy, is God really watching me?' He wanted to get his doctrine correct!

My son said, 'William, it's true, God is watching you

because He loves you so much He can't take His eyes off of you.'

God *is* watching you tonight—you who have surrendered your life to Jesus Christ, you who have submitted yourself to the lordship of Jesus Christ. He is watching you tonight because He loves you so much He can't take His eyes off of you.

He is for you. He has made all of His infinite resources available for us. He's placed them at our disposal. If God is for us, who can be against us?

There are forces and powers in this world that *are* against us. The Bible speaks of the world and the flesh and the devil as they work in concert against us. All three together, working in concert, make a formidable foe, greater than I can personally withstand. I cannot stand against the forces of the world, the flesh and the devil— but my God can, and does, and will in me!

'Who shall lay anything to the charge of God's elect?'

Well, I'll tell you, there is somebody who is constantly making accusations and charges: the devil, 'the accuser of our brethren... which accused them before our God day and night' (Rev 12:10).

Never think he's your friend. We read in Job of him acting as the accuser of the brethren. The sons of God were presenting themselves to God, and Satan also came with them, and God said to Satan, 'Have you considered My servant Job?'

The word 'considered' has, in the Hebrew, the associations of a general who is planning to attack a city, and he is creating his strategy; he's looking at the city, watching when they open the gates, how they open, when they close; determining the strategy for attack, so that he might take that city. It's a military term.

Satan accused Job of being a mercenary: 'Yes, I've seen

that fellow and I've seen also how You've blessed him. Job is a mercenary, Lord. You've put a fence around him, You won't let me get to him, and the way You've blessed him, hey, anybody would serve You, blessed like that—a man would have to be crazy not to serve You. Let me take away...'

But when I have surrendered to the lordship of Jesus Christ, though the enemy may accuse me, the glorious thing is that God is not accusing or laying anything to my charge. If you have surrendered to the lordship of Christ, God has justified you of all that you have ever done.

That word 'justified' goes a step beyond forgiveness. It means 'just as though it had never happened'. God has so obliterated your past that he has wiped out your past. He has justified you. He is not receiving any charges against you.

'Who is he that condemneth?'

How often Satan takes advantage of our weaknesses to bring us into condemnation and to make us feel unworthy of coming to God. I look at my life and I say, 'God, I wouldn't blame you for just throwing me aside.' And Satan loves to come at a time when I have failed and tell me how undeserving and unworthy I am of God's love.

You know, I used to listen to him. And I used to get so defeated, looking at my life and looking at the failures in my life, when Satan would come along and start this heavy trip of condemnation.

But I've gotten wise to him. As Martin Luther said, 'When Satan comes to me and says, "Martin Luther, you are not deserving the love or the goodness of God, God ought to just cast you out of the kingdom, you are not worthy of even calling upon Him, you should just go away and hide," ' Martin Luther said, 'I answer and say, "Satan, what you say is correct. However, you do not drive me away from God, but you only drive me to the cross of Jesus Christ wherein is my only hope." '

There is a difference between the conviction of the Holy Spirit and the condemnation of Satan, but it's very easy to discern between the two, if you know the secret. A lot of people don't, and they just let Satan beat them into a state of total defeat. And Satan comes as an angel of light; he may even like you to think that this is the Spirit of God just telling you how evil and horrible and rotten you are.

But it's easy to tell the difference. When Satan is condemning you the result is that you want to hide from God. But when the Holy Spirit is convicting you, you can't wait to get to God to get it all over with. The Holy Spirit is always drawing you unto God, and that's the purpose of the conviction of the Spirit—to draw me unto God, to get that thing over with, to get it wiped out. Whereas the effect of the condemnation of Satan is to push me away from Him.

Some of you have been allowing Satan to condemn you; you're condemning yourselves. 'Who is he that condemneth?' Let me tell you something. I know one who is not condemning you, and that is Jesus Christ our Lord.

He said to Nicodemus, 'For God did not send his Son into the world to condemn the world, but that the world through him might be saved. And he that believeth is not condemned.'

He didn't come to condemn. That wasn't the purpose of His coming. The purpose of His coming was to save. One day they brought to Him a woman taken in the very act of adultery. 'Lord, our law says stone her. What do You say?'

I find something rather interesting in this. First of all, if they caught her in the very act, where was the man? The law said stone them both. But Jesus said, 'I say unto you, let he who is without sin cast the first stone,' and then He knelt down and began with His finger to write in the dust.

The Bible doesn't tell us what Jesus wrote. But I would like to offer a suggestion. It's not biblically provable, it's not meant to create a doctrine. But I think He wrote the names of individuals in the crowd, and against those names, sins they had committed that nobody else knew of. And one by one, from the eldest to the least, they all left, and Jesus stood up and said, 'What happened to your accusers?' And she said, 'Well, Lord, I guess I don't have any.' And what did He say? 'Neither do I condemn you.'

Jesus isn't condemning us. He died for our sins. He has risen again, and He is even at the right hand of the Father making intercession for us. The Father is the Judge; His Son is our Solicitor. This is glorious! The Father will not receive any accusations against me. And the Son is there as my Intercessor, my Advocate with the Father.

'Who, then, shall separate us from the love of Christ?'

When you surrender yourself to the lordship of Jesus Christ, there is no power in heaven or earth that can separate you from that love that He has for you. 'Shall tribulation, or distress, or persecution, or famine, or nakedness, or peril, or sword?... Nay, in all these things we are more than conquerors through him that loved us.'

Now, I've always wondered what is 'more than conqueror'. I know what being a conqueror is. But what is it to be more than a conqueror?

To be a conqueror is to have victory over the opposition. But often you don't know if you're a conqueror or not until those last few seconds. That's what makes sport such an exciting activity to watch. But to be more than conqueror is to have the victory in the midst of the battle. And when I go into a battle I have the victory even in the midst of the conflict, because of Jesus Christ and His power within.

You see, in the great conflict against the enemy the interesting thing about the conflict is that the end is already a decided matter. Jesus Christ has triumphed over those forces and powers of darkness and, as we heard tonight, we see Jesus. He was made a little lower than angels for the suffering of death, but we see Him crowned with glory and honour—and the ultimate triumph belongs to Jesus Christ our Lord, and in Him I have victory. The ultimate triumph is mine in Christ.

So it isn't a question of the outcome at all; the outcome is assured—I am more than a conqueror through Him that loves me—and I need to remember that, when I go into these issues of life where I am under pressure, when the enemy seems to come in and I begin to despair. I need to realise that Christ is my victory and in Him I am more than a conqueror.

Oh, how glorious it is to know Jesus Christ as Lord, to have this relationship now with God, where my sin issue is completely settled and where I have that assurance in life! 'For I am persuaded, that neither death, nor life, nor angels, nor principalities, nor powers, nor things present, nor things to come, nor height, nor depth, nor any other creature, shall be able to separate me from the love of God, which is in Christ Jesus our Lord.'

Oh, how wise it is to choose to surrender your life to the lordship of Jesus Christ! Because all that you need to successfully run the race and win is imparted to you by your loving Father, the moment you submit to His lordship. Surely that is the choice, the wisest choice any of us could ever make!

KEEP IN STEP WITH THE SPIRIT

by Rev. Donald Bridge

Galatians 5:25

One of the questions that tends to divide godly believers concerns the work of the Holy Spirit. How is He manifested, how is He displayed, how is He evidenced? Does He make Himself felt and known? If so, how? Indeed, should He be manifested at all in seen and felt ways, or is it more correct to speak (as some devout people have always spoken) of the Holy Spirit as 'the almost anonymous person of the Trinity', who never seems to draw attention to Himself, and constantly loves to point to Jesus?

Now, which is it? Is He anonymous, or is He manifested? Is He seen, or unseen? The answer, so often, is surely, 'neither at one end nor in the middle, but at both ends and in the middle at once'.

We have the authority of Jesus Himself for comparing the Holy Spirit to the wind. And we have those familiar words from John 3:8: 'The wind blows where it wishes. You hear the sound of it but you cannot tell where it comes from or where it goes to. So is everyone that is born of the Spirit.'

I am very interested in wind because I love sailing. When you go sailing, one of the most obvious things about the wind is of course that it is invisible, as Jesus was saying.

I have never once seen the wind, and yet the wind is the one essential ingredient, apart from the boat, for sailing. I have never seen it but I have often seen and felt its effect. The boom swings over when you jib without intending to, and wallops you over the back of the head. the tiller, the rudder, the centre-board and the sail all pull and counter-pull at the wind's touch; the boat heels over and you hang out in that marvellous way that does a world of good to slipped discs; you can see a squall approaching as a swiftly moving ruffle over the water—but I've never seen the wind.

If we only believe in what we can see, then one would have to say there is no reason to believe that the wind exists! And yet we know that's an absurd statement. The wind is unseen but felt, manifested and evidenced.

'You don't see where it comes from,' said Jesus, 'but you do hear the sound of it; so it is with the Holy Spirit.' What He does is evident and recognisable and manifested, though He Himself is both invisible and—yes, amazingly, divinely modest. He does not draw attention to Himself.

In our reading from Galatians chapter 5, verse 16 onwards, we have some vivid, suggestive and challenging descriptions of some of the works of the Holy Spirit—evidence of His invisible presence. In this little section there is a key phrase, subdivided and expanded into three commands.

'Live by the Spirit'

'Live by the Spirit.' Make the will of the divine Spirit, that lovely, gentle, powerful, gracious, holy, divine person—make His will your principle of life. May He be your motivating power. Every virtue we possess and every victory known, every thought of holiness, are His alone.

People have talked to me and sought counsel from me this week who seem to feel, themselves, some reservations about whether the Spirit of God is really at work in their lives, because there is not some particular manifestation. But as I have stood and listened to them and talked to them, I have wanted to laugh, as I've had to say to them, 'But I can see the Spirit working in your life. Where do you think those holy desires come from? Where do you think that anxiety comes from? Who do you think has led you to say, "Tonight, tonight I must nail it down and be right with God and leave this tent knowing that I am right with Him" '?

Who put that into your mind—the world? the flesh? the devil? I very much doubt it. The Holy Spirit did. 'Live by the Spirit'—and if you ask 'What in detail does that mean? how do I go about it?', the second half of the verse goes on, by contrast, to tell us that, by implication, if you live by the Spirit you will not gratify the desires of the sinful nature.

Then what *will* you gratify? You will gratify the desires of His holy nature, instead of gratifying the desires of your sinful nature. And this is exactly what verse 17 goes on to say. 'For the sinful nature desires what is contrary to the Spirit, and the Spirit what is contrary to the sinful nature. They are in conflict with each other, so that you do not do what you want.'

Gratify the Spirit's desires, give in to His wishes, bow to His will, surrender to His influence. Of course, there's a strong implication of conflict there—it says so, doesn't it; conflict words are used. We don't just float along on a wave of ecstasy when we live in the Spirit.

Somebody said to me very recently, 'Since I became a Christian, I feel temptation much more than I used to before. What's the matter with me?'

My reply was, 'Well, of course you do. Previously you

hardly felt it because you hardly fought it—and you didn't fight it because the Spirit of God wasn't within you to give you the motive to fight it.'

Jesus fought temptation, not less, but more, than anyone else. He is the only one who never succumbed to it; holy, harmless, undefiled, tempted in all points as we are, yet without sin. So make the Spirit of God not a neglected half-welcome Guest to whom you give a kind of acknowledgement in a theological doffing of your hat—'Well, yes, when I came to Jesus I was born again—I wasn't aware of it at the time, but I realise now that when I came to Jesus I was born again by the Holy Spirit, so He must live in me.'

That is perfectly true, perfectly true. But surely we can make a little more of Him than that!—more than simply saying, 'Well, yes, I didn't notice at the time, but I was born again of the Spirit.' He is a divine Guest, so honoured and respected and consciously welcomed, whose every wish is so eagerly followed, that when people begin to wonder, 'Who is the guest and who is the host?', we begin to realise that the whole thing is turning round and we are now the guests in His life so to speak.

'Choose seven men filled with the Spirit,' they said in Acts chapter 6, at a time when church growth, evangelism, and expansion brought difficulties and conflict. Somebody said to me recently, 'We've got enough problems in our church without having church growth as well.' And there can be problems.

So what did the early church do to meet the church growth situation? They grew, they expanded their bureaucracy in a sense, they appointed what may have been the first deacons. How did they appoint them? 'Choose seven men filled with the Spirit.'

That's interesting; it's not 'choose seven men who keep

telling you that they've been filled with the Spirit, and keep telling you all about their marvellous experiences.' No. 'Choose seven people whom you have observed to be filled with the Spirit, whom you know to be filled with the Spirit.'

Somebody came to me after a Bible rally and said to me, 'Tell me, Mr Bridge, I'm almost sure you're born again, aren't you, even though you are a Baptist minister?' And I said, 'Well, yes, I am, actually, yes.' She said, 'Yes, I think you're well saved, aren't you?' And I said, 'Well, I suppose I must be; because I'm certainly saved, and I was saved by God, and God does things well—so yes, I'm well saved.' And then she looked very arch and she said, 'Have you been filled with the Holy Spirit?'

I was a little bit naughty, because I'm sure I could have said 'yes' in her terms. But the conversation irritated me a little and so I deliberately looked puzzled. I said, 'Well, you're asking the wrong person. Go and ask other people.' She said, 'But I'm asking you.' I replied: 'Well, I can't find anywhere in the New Testament where people say, "I have been filled with the Holy Spirit." I find over and over again that the comment is made by others, or by God Himself, "He was filled with the Holy Spirit." '

So I said, 'You go and ask some other people who know me. Ask them if they observe that I am filled with the Holy Spirit.'

'Live by the Spirit.' That, then, is our principal command, and then there are three outworkings, or expansions, of what that involves. Verse 18: 'Be led by the Spirit.' That speaks of His guidance. Verse 22: 'Grow in the Spirit.' That speaks of His fruit. Verse 25: 'Keep in step with the Spirit.' That speaks of His energetic progress. What a job it is to keep up with Him!

Be Led by the Spirit

Certainly leading in the sense of specific guidance is included. People have sought help from preachers and counsellors this week, in some cases because they need to know which turning to take next, which door to go through. They are sensing that God is moving them forward.

And I've no doubt at all that if you are led by the Spirit, you're not under that legalistic bondage; without a doubt it included the Spirit leading us in matters of career, of marriage, of personal problems, of difficult decisions, of a calling to some work for God, an opportunity to witness for Christ, a prompting to pray. The last very specially that: when the Holy Spirit prompts you to pray for someone, or pray for something, pray, pray.

Respond to His promptings; yes, I'm sure it includes that. It may well include from time to time very striking 'coincidences'. An occasional vision—a wise or prophetic word from a fellow Christian—a sermon that is astonishingly relevant, though the preacher has no idea how relevant it is—a Bible text that leaps out and grabs you—a breathless stillness as the presence of God is deeply felt in your personal prayer time.

Oh yes, manifestations, as Paul would call them, often experienced by Christians.

But I must put to you, very gently, that the specific and strongest meaning of the word 'led' isn't all those lovely and exciting things. It is a word of much wider meaning, more diffuse. It simply means 'prompted', or 'pushed along'. It's a picture of an instinctive leaning that is scarcely thought through on the conscious level at all. The whole picture is one of a general course of life, a direction taken, a development of new instincts and leanings, a willingness—indeed, an eagerness—to ask of any proposed step, 'Can I unashamedly ask Jesus to join me in this? Can I unhesitantly invite Jesus to join me in this?'

I remember a young man at Frinton, when many, many young men and older ones were being converted, and still are, in that marvellous church there. Long after his conversion, this particular young man still insisted on wearing a particular kind of leather jacket which had on it the logo of a heavy rock group known to be deep into sexual deviation and the occult. He wore his jacket and played the group's records. On my own son's advice (he was of the same age group) I was unwilling to baptise that lad until he was unwilling to wear that jacket.

That might sound somewhat pharisaical, and a little bit external, and all the rest of it, but it seemed to me there was a contradiction between what he was wearing, and his claim to be walking in the Spirit of God.

I've heard excellent news of that lad since. He's not a lad now. He's got there, he's going places with God. But at that time I believe there was a very real hesitation.

Could you invite Jesus to wear that leather jacket—not because it's leather but because of the logo on it and what it stands for? You could invite Jesus to mix with those people—He did, constantly, and shocked others by doing it. But I don't think He'd have worn that logo.

Grow in the Spirit

Secondly, verse 22, the fruit of the Spirit: 'The fruit of the Spirit is love, joy, peace, patience, kindness, goodness, faithfulness, gentleness, self-control.'

I've called that 'growing in the Spirit', because, in using that vivid metaphor of 'fruit' or 'harvest', Paul is clearly implying at least two things; the idea of patience and the idea of cultivation.

First of all, *patience*. You see, fruit does not suddenly appear; and it is fruit which, moved by the Spirit of God,

Paul takes as the metaphor of this work of the Spirit. A decision to trust Christ and follow Him may be sudden—not in every case, but it may be. The discovery of a spiritual gift can be swift too, though very often it needs careful training. But fruit takes rather longer. There's no such thing as fast fruit.

After Keswick 1989, what matters is not how you're going to feel the Monday after the Convention finishes. It's what you and I are, say, in 1990 and 1995, if our Saviour hasn't returned. It's not what we feel in the circles and ups and downs that make up our human experiences. All the time fruit is taking a while to grow, and it's not what we feel like next Monday (though that tends to matter terribly to us) it's what we are the Monday after that, the Wednesday after that, a year after that: what we become.

The second thought about fruit is that, of course, you don't just wait for fruit, you *cultivate* it. And that is why it is vitally important to decide on the books we read and the films we watch and the friendships we cultivate—yes, that very word—and the habits we train ourselves in; the things we say 'yes' to and the things we say 'no' to, the company we keep and the seriousness, above all, with which we regularly, persistently, whether we feel like it or not, get into the word of God.

We are to cultivate the growing of the fruit. God alone can make it grow, but we are giving a hand in its cultivation.

Do you long for a heart harvest? Do you long to be a person marked by love, joy, peace, patience, kindness, goodness, faithfulness, gentleness, self-control? Well, the very fact that you long to be like that is at least the evidence of the beginning of a work of the Holy Spirit in your life. And it takes time. But make Him welcome—

make Him welcome. Hand over to Him and get on with your cultivating.

Keep in step with the Spirit

Thirdly, verse 25: 'Keep in step with the Spirit.'

That's a great phrase. The NIV would be worth buying for that phrase alone! The Authorised Version has 'walk in the Spirit', as indeed it does in verse 16, but they are actually two different words. The Revised Standard Version has 'walk by the Spirit' here in verse 25—slightly more suggestive of our involvement in it. The Good News Bible paraphrases it, and I think drops back somewhat in the meaning, by saying 'the Spirit must control our lives', though that's perfectly true of course. The New English Bible has 'let the Spirit direct your course', but my disappointment with those last two paraphrases is that they make the thrust of it rather more passive than Paul is saying. It isn't just 'let Him', it is 'step in with Him'.

The NIV reading seems to me to be the best of them all. Because the flavour of the Greek here is not merely 'being moved along' almost passively, as in 'led by the Spirit' that we have seen already. It's a word that would be used, for example, in a military context, 'forming fours', 'stepping out in full battle kit'; or a political context, 'getting into line with Cabinet decisions'. We are invited to get in line with the Holy Spirit; to accept a Cabinet reshuffle that makes it doubly clear that He's in the chair, and to make decisions, take steps and initiate actions that willingly, freely, are in accord with what the Holy Spirit wants to do.

It's not only surrendering to Him—though that comes first—but it's going with Him. He is today most surely on the move. We are living in a day of the Spirit of God. And so the NIV brilliantly translates, 'keep in step with the Spirit'. You see, that gives the sense of changing step if necessary—getting in line—forming fours—getting on your military kit—moving with Him.

It takes some doing, it takes some keeping up with. We'll get out of breath at times. There will be times when He will say, like Jesus said to Peter in that glorious story in Luke chapter 5, 'Drop your nets out there,' and you will be tempted to reply, as quite clearly Peter very nearly replied, 'Look, which of us is the carpenter and which is the fisherman?'—but he then took another look into the eyes of Jesus and said, 'But nevertheless—although that's the first thought that comes to me—nevertheless, if You say so—if You say so—I'll do it Your way.'

He'll sometimes say, like the Spirit said to Peter on the rooftop, in Acts chapter 10 there, 'Go with those folk that are knocking on the door now,' and you'll have to stop saying, 'Well, Lord, they're not my type actually,' because you've just learned that you can't say, 'Not so, Lord.' You can say, 'Not so,' in which case He's not Lord, or you can say, 'Lord,' in which case you abandon saying, 'Not so.' It's one or the other.

It won't be a once-and-for-all second blessing, it's an on-and-on experience. Keep on being filled with the Spirit. Keep on walking in the Spirit. Keep on keeping step with the Spirit. Keep up with Him by His grace.

Is the Holy Spirit in a little attic of your life somewhere? Well, let me tell you, He's planning to be the Managing Director! He's planning a takeover, and He'll accept nothing else. But it's not a forcible one. He invites you to say, 'Yes, Lord, take over. I will join the takeover bid willingly. I will use my vote as a shareholder and say, I want to be under new management. I want to be under dynamic management. I want to be under all-knowing management. I want to be under holy management. Spirit of God, I invite You, make You welcome—You who have already given me new life and are already the Guest within. Holy Spirit of God, I'd rather be the guest, I'd rather You were the host. Will You come out of the attic, where my neglect and my disobedience and my doubts have often kept You? I see now that You've been watching me, and now I say, come down into the forecourt of the hotel again, come down to the desk where it all begins, and I'll hand over the keys to You. Holy Spirit of God, I want to walk with You, I want to know You better, I want to follow in Your steps, I want to be led by You, I want to be changed by You, I want to keep in step with You. Spirit of God, fill me.'

KESWICK 1989 TAPES AND VIDEOS

Tapes
Here is a list of tape numbers for all the messages in this book.
The numbers follow the sequence in the book.

The Bible Readings
Rev. Philip Hacking: 89/2, 89/3, 89/4, 89/5
Rev. Chuck Smith: 89/26, 89/27, 89/28, 89/29

The Addresses

Rev. David Jackman	89/1
Canon Keith Weston	89/15
Mr Peter Maiden	89/16
Rev. Jim Graham	89/18
Mr Victor Jack	89/20
Rev. Robert Amess	89/31
Rev. George Hoffman	89/32
Rev. Philip Hacking	89/34
Rev. Chuck Smith	89/36
Rev. Donald Bridge	89/38

These tapes, together with a full list of Keswick tapes, can be obtained from:
International Christian Communications
4 Regency Mews
Silverdale Road
Eastbourne
East Sussex
BN20 7AB.

Videos
The addresses in this book (with one exception[1]) are available on video. To order, send your remittance (£19.95 sterling for each set of Bible Readings, £9.95 for individual addresses, plus £2.50 p&p, cheques payable to Bagster Video Ltd.) to Keswick Convention Video Tape Ministries, PO Box 700, Alton, Hampshire, England, or write for further details.

[1] The only address not included is the one by Rev. David Jackman, p. 143.

KESWICK 1990

The annual Keswick Convention takes place each July at the heart of England's beautiful Lake District. The two separate weeks of the Convention offer an unparalleled opportunity for listening to gifted Bible exposition, experiencing Christian fellowship with believers from all over the world, and enjoying something of the unspoilt grandeur of God's creation.

Each of the two weeks has a series of four morning Bible readings, followed by other messages throughout the rest of the day. The programme in the second week is a little less intensive, and it is often referred to as 'Holiday Week'. There are also regular meetings throughout the fortnight for young people, and in the second week for children.

The dates for the 1990 Keswick Convention are 14–21 July and 21–28 July. The Bible Reading speakers are Bishop Michael Baughen and Mr Charles Price. Other speakers during the fortnight are Warren Wiersbe, Billy Strachan, Michael Wilcock, Hugh Palmer, Keith White, Ian Knox, Philip Hacking, Alex Ross, Ian Barclay and Ian Coffey.

Further details may be obtained from:

The Keswick Convention Secretary
PO Box 292
Harrow
Middlesex
HA1 2NP